"Bravo, Schiraldi! *The Adverse Childhood Experiences Recovery Workbook* carefully guides survivors through the process of understanding and healing from childhood wounds. It is carefully organized to maximize skills learning and practice, and to minimize potential overwhelm when confronting painful feelings and memories. After working through behavior generated from past experiences, the workbook also helps users apply these learnings to disturbing recent or current events. Designed for independent 'self-help,' some survivors may choose to use this comprehensive adverse childhood experiences (ACEs) recovery workbook in the context of a therapeutic relationship."

—**Esther Giller**, president of the Sidran Institute

"As one who has treated trauma for many years, I have always thought that what happens in our childhood directly impacts our mental and physical health in the now. I recommend Glenn Schiraldi's workbook to educate you about the impact of ACEs on your present well-being, and the many effective paths to heal those hidden wounds from earlier times that still affect you."

—**Laney Rosenzweig, MS, LMFT**, developer of accelerated resolution therapy (ART)

"An integrative approach to healing from traumatic stress that targets mind, brain, body, and soul, this workbook will be an important resource for many who struggle with the lasting imprints of adverse early experiences."

—**Ruth A. Lanius, MD, PhD**, professor of psychiatry, Harris-Woodman Chair in Mind-Body Medicine, and director of the posttraumatic stress disorder (PTSD) research unit at the University of Western Ontario

"Glenn Schiraldi has provided a much-needed guide for those who have experienced childhood maltreatment in one form or another. He painstakingly discusses in easy-to-understand terms the psychological and medical consequences of early-life trauma, and outlines a series of interventions ranging from trauma-focused therapy to nutrition, exercise, and mindfulness/meditation. This will be helpful to patients, families, and students, as well as the broad spectrum of mental health professionals who deal with adult victims of childhood maltreatment daily."

—**Charles B. Nemeroff, MD, PhD**, Matthew P. Nemeroff Endowed Chair in the department of psychiatry and behavioral sciences at the Mulva Clinic for the Neurosciences, and director of the Institute for Early Life Adversity Research at The University of Texas at Austin Dell Medical School

"Drawing on his own rich and diverse background and inspired by a variety of treatment approaches, Glenn Schiraldi has gifted the world a workbook that is destined to be an essential resource for those who have experienced ACEs, which includes nearly everyone. This engaging, accessible volume is filled with diverse, creative exercises that guide the reader to safely revisit and heal the effects of the past on brain and body—all the while imparting hope and confidence that dreams of a future that is free of the constraints of the past can become a lived reality."

—**Pat Ogden, PhD**, developer of sensorimotor psychotherapy, author of *Sensorimotor Psychotherapy*, and coauthor of *Trauma and the Body*

The Adverse Childhood Experiences Recovery Workbook

Heal the Hidden Wounds *from* Childhood Affecting
Your Adult Mental *and* Physical Health

GLENN R. SCHIRALDI, PhD

New Harbinger Publications, Inc.

Publisher's Note

This publication is designed to provide helpful information on the subject addressed. It is not intended to substitute for needed professional help. If expert assistance or counseling is needed, the services of a competent professional should be sought. Unless full names are given, names in the cases herein are changed or reflect composites.

Distributed in Canada by Raincoast Books

Copyright © 2021 by Glenn R. Schiraldi
      New Harbinger Publications, Inc.
      5674 Shattuck Avenue
      Oakland, CA 94609
      www.newharbinger.com

Image of father napping with daughter is reprinted with permission of Megan Warren, Starry Night Art Studio, Fullerton, CA. © 2018 Megan Warren.

Image of mother smiling at child is © Photographer / Stockfresh.
Used with permission

"Loving the Body Meditation" from *Guilt is the Teacher, Love is the Lesson* by Joan Borysenko PhD., copyright ©1990. Reprinted by permission of Grand Central Publishing, an imprint of Hachette Book Group, Inc.

"Life's Accomplishments and Internal Resources Exercise" reprinted with permission of James D. Fouts. © 1990.

Cover design by Amy Shoup; Acquired by Tesilya Hanauer; Edited by Karen Levy

---

Library of Congress Cataloging-in-Publication Data

Names: Schiraldi, Glenn R., 1947- author.

Title: The adverse childhood experiences recovery workbook : heal the hidden wounds from childhood affecting your adult mental and physical health / Glenn Schiraldi.

Description: Oakland, CA : New Harbinger Publications, [2020] | Includes bibliographical references.

Identifiers: LCCN 2020022399 (print) | LCCN 2020022400 (ebook) | ISBN 9781684036646 (trade paperback) | ISBN 9781684036653 (pdf) | ISBN 9781684036660 (epub)

Subjects: LCSH: Adult child abuse victims--Rehabilitation--Problems, exercises, etc. | Psychic trauma--Treatment--Problems, exercises, etc.

Classification: LCC RC569.5.C55 S37 2020 (print) | LCC RC569.5.C55 (ebook) | DDC 616.85/822390651--dc23

LC record available at https://lccn.loc.gov/2020022399

LC ebook record available at https://lccn.loc.gov/2020022400

Printed in the United States of America

23   22

10   9   8   7   6   5   4   3   2

Sorrow prepares you for joy. It violently sweeps everything out of your house, so that new joy can find space to enter. It shakes the yellow leaves from the bough of your heart, so that fresh, green leaves can grow in their place. It pulls up the rotten roots, so that new roots hidden beneath have room to grow. Whatever sorrow shakes from your heart, far better things will take their place.

—Jalaluddin Rumi

Contents

Introduction

Life is hard. It is supposed to be. Although we would never wish suffering on anyone we love, without it we would never develop the confidence to overcome adversity. We would never learn how to heal, and thus be useful to ourselves and to others. Many of us, however, have experienced especially difficult challenges. Whether it's abuse, neglect, or living in a troubled home, the toxic stress of adverse childhood experiences (ACEs) affects every community. If unresolved, it imprints and changes the brain, biology, and sense of self in ways that can affect our well-being throughout our lives and even from one generation to later generations. ACEs may well be called the number-one unaddressed public health concern because of the devastation they leave in their wake.

Fortunately, toxic childhood stress *can be resolved*. This workbook will guide you to heal the inner wounds caused by your ACEs and build the life you desire. This workbook is about hope and taking responsibility for your well-being. You'll find it healing to understand your challenges—the adversity you face and have faced. It will be comforting to realize there are reasons for your suffering. The reasons make sense. You are not crazy or abnormal. You'll realize that there are many healing options, even if you are an older adult. This workbook will help you address the root causes of your hidden wounds, rather than ignoring or hiding from these causes.

This workbook is not about blaming problems on the past. Blaming only makes us feel like helpless victims. Nor is it about judging anyone—your parents or yourself, who, like all of us, did what we knew to do at the time. Harsh judgments and criticism just keep us stuck in bitterness and deflate motivation. Rather, this workbook is about seeing new possibilities and solutions for healing that you can actively pursue. If willpower alone has not worked as well as you'd like, this workbook will provide many more healing options.

Why This Workbook?

We now know that the way we experience ourselves profoundly influences our overall psychological health and functioning. Trying to change this experience by focusing on present thought patterns alone is typically ineffective. What is needed is a new approach—one that directly addresses hidden wounds from the past at a deeper level. Over the course of this workbook, you'll learn how to transform suffering and shame, which often originate in the early years and exist below the level of conscious awareness, into a secure and wholesome sense of self. You'll bring into the light of day the felt sense—the wordless discomfort that you can't seem to shake, the feeling that something is wrong with you—and replace these feelings with a quiet inner gladness to be who you are.

In addition to healing hidden wounds from the early years, you can reasonably expect that the skills in this workbook will improve your mental and physical health generally (Weinberg 2013). As you bring your whole (healed) self to the present, you'll more fully enjoy life and be more fully there for yourself and those you care about.

How to Get the Most from This Workbook

This workbook is about practicing and mastering skills, because knowledge alone is not sufficient to change your brain. The workbook follows a logical sequence. Each skill builds on the skills that precede it. You might wish to skip around. However, you'll likely get the most benefit from working your way through this workbook from front to back, getting reasonably good at each skill before moving on to the next. There are also materials available for download at the website for this book: http://www.newharbinger.com/46646. (See the very back of this book for more details.)

How This Workbook Is Organized

In Part I, you'll learn how the toxic stress of ACEs harms your body and emotional health, and how loving bonds in childhood help the brain develop properly.

Part II will very effectively guide you on your healing journey. Chapter 4 explains why there is much cause to hope for healing from ACEs. We've learned so much in recent years about traumatic memories and how to heal them, both through our own efforts and, as needed, with the help of a capable mental health professional.

Chapters 5, 6, and 7 strengthen your brain and prepare it for your healing journey. Chapters 5 and 6 will teach you how to regulate stress and strong distressing emotions so that your brain can function at its best. Chapter 7 will show you the keys to optimizing brain health, function, and mood—preparing your brain to rapidly rewire in healthy ways.

Nurturing imagery simulates the loving attachment bonds that promote proper brain development. Chapters 8 through 11 will guide you to create new nurturing experiences—experiences that were needed but probably lacking in your early years. Sometimes providing needed nurturing from imagined ideal care-givers and sometimes from yourself, these imagery experiences create constructive neural patterns in the brain that begin to offset disturbing brain wiring resulting from ACEs. Newly formed neural pathways will help you feel and function at your best. In chapter 12, you'll begin to grow the pattern of soothing difficult experiences with comfort, protection, and encouragement. The skills you'll have learned up to this point will prepare you to address and heal your earliest wounds as you move ahead.

In chapters 13 and 14 you'll learn how to trace disturbing recent events or thoughts to childhood events that influence your present life. You'll learn how to settle both the recent events and the old wounds.

Shame is at the core of so much suffering in survivors of ACEs. Chapters 15 through 23 go to the heart of your suffering, showing you how to replace painful shame with inner security and a quiet gladness to be you.

Everyone will suffer, but there is more to life than suffering and even more than healing. Chapters 24 through 28 will show you ways to transition beyond healing to create a satisfying and joyful life.

Finally, chapter 29 will give you an opportunity to consider the principles and skills that have helped you the most, and create a plan to keep your skills sharp throughout your life's journey.

My desire is that you become a master healer and an expert in developing your best possible health—a wholesome sense of self, inner security, and feeling good. These are the goals of this workbook. Take the time you need. The healing journey is worth your time and effort. Go at your own pace. If any part of this workbook becomes overwhelming, put it aside for a while. Use the calming skills you'll learn. Perhaps you'll wish to find a capable mental health professional to support you in your healing journey. Let's begin this journey together.

PART I

About Adverse Childhood Experiences

CHAPTER 1

Toxic Stress and Adverse Childhood Experiences

Each of us has usually experienced three kinds of stress: good stress, tolerable stress, and toxic stress (McEwen 2017). Each can cause us to stretch and grow, but toxic stress presents unique challenges, especially in childhood. These kinds of stress exist on a continuum, meaning that the line between them is somewhat gradual, but they can generally be defined as follows.

- *Good stress* challenges without overwhelming us. We are under control emotionally and tend to make good decisions. Think of a student who has prepared for an important exam or a prepared athlete performing well in a big game. The stress response—fight or flight—is brief, and levels of stress hormones are appropriate.

- *Tolerable stress* might involve intense fight-or-flight physical changes, with greater elevations of stress hormones. However, the body eventually returns to normal, especially if trusted adults help the child buffer the stress. Recovery occurs before there is lasting physical or psychological damage. For example, you might think of the death of a loved one from natural causes or a community coming together after a hurricane.

- *Toxic stress* is so overwhelming, so severe or chronic, that a person is "shook up" and stressed for a long time. This kind of stress adversely affects the brain and biology in ways that impair adult health, work performance, relationships, judgment, impulse control, spirituality, and self-esteem—especially in the absence of a safe adult to buffer the stress. The effects of toxic stress can be passed down intergenerationally if unchecked.

This brings us to a fascinating line of research regarding toxic early life stress.

The Adverse Childhood Experiences Study

The Adverse Childhood Experiences (ACEs) Study is the brainchild of two medical doctors, Vincent Felitti, head of Kaiser Permanente's Department of Preventive Medicine in San Diego, California, and Robert Anda, a Centers for Disease Control and Prevention researcher (Felitti 2002). Analyzing the medical records of more than 17,000 everyday patients at a large health maintenance organization, they found that ten commonly reported ACEs predict a very wide range of psychological, medical, and functional problems. The ten ACEs are:

- **Three kinds of abuse**
  - Sexual
  - Physical
  - Emotional

- **Two kinds of neglect**
  - Emotional
  - Physical

- **Five kinds of household dysfunction**
  - Parents divorced or separated
  - Witnessing a mother or stepmother being treated violently
  - A household member addicted to alcohol or other drugs
  - A household member suicidal or mentally ill
  - A household member in jail

Felitti and Anda (2014) found that about two-thirds of adults had experienced at least one of these early life adversities. And ACEs didn't usually occur in isolation: most who had experienced one ACE also had experienced at least one more. For example, an alcoholic father might also be abusive.

Dis-*orders*—departures from our usual order—often have multiple causes, such as infection, a toxic physical environment, lack of social support, unhealthy lifestyle, genes, and temperament. However, Felitti and Anda's original study and scores of later studies have shown that ACEs independently predict many disorders, and do so in a stepwise fashion. That is, the higher one's ACEs score, the greater the likelihood of developing a disorder. Here is a sampling of what ACEs predict.

- **Medical Conditions**
  - Obesity (eating might self-medicate pain; "Maybe people will leave me alone if I'm unattractive or if I can throw my weight around")
  - Type 2 diabetes
  - Cardiovascular disease (heart disease, stroke)
  - Cancer

- Pain

- Autoimmune diseases (rheumatoid arthritis, type 1 diabetes, multiple sclerosis, lupus, psoriasis, celiac disease, inflammatory bowel disease, Graves' disease, vitiligo, idiopathic pulmonary fibrosis, primary biliary cirrhosis)

- Fibromyalgia

- Chronic fatigue

- Hepatitis

- Nearly all sleep disorders (sleep apnea, nightmares, insomnia, narcolepsy, sleepwalking, sleep eating)

- Reproductive problems (sexually transmitted diseases, preterm birth)

- Ulcers

- Fractures

- Shorter life span (by nearly twenty years when ACE score is 6 or higher)

- Poorer self-rated health

- **Mental Health Conditions**

  - Low self-esteem

  - Depression (including bipolar disorder)

  - Anxiety (including panic disorder)

  - Post-traumatic stress disorder (PTSD) and complex PTSD

  - Borderline personality disorder

  - Attention deficit hyperactivity disorder (ADHD)

- **Risky Behaviors**

  - Drug abuse or misuse (smoking, substance use disorder, injecting drugs intravenously, misusing prescription drugs—taking too much or too often or using them without a prescription, using a higher number of prescriptions)

  - Suicide attempts

  - Precocious sexual activity (greater likelihood of intercourse by age fifteen, having multiple sex partners, teen paternity and maternity, unintended pregnancy)

  - Intimate partner violence (greater likelihood of victimization or perpetration, including later being raped)

- Physical inactivity

- Criminality

- **Impaired Functioning**

  - Occupational or financial challenges (serious problems performing one's job or concentrating, absenteeism, serious financial problems, lower lifetime income)

  - Memory disturbance

  - More marriages

  - Lower educational attainment

How strongly do ACEs predict these conditions? At an ACE score of four or more, compared with zero, the risks typically increase two to five times. The risks are even higher for alcoholism (seven-fold increase), suicide attempts (twelve-fold increase), and learning and behavioral problems (up to a thirty-three-fold increase for problems including ADHD, which is often misdiagnosed as bipolar disorder). Individual ACEs are about equal in their ability to cause damage.

The initial trauma of a young child may go underground, but it will return to haunt us.
—James Garbarino

ACE research has led to the following conclusions:

- ACEs are cumulative risk factors for seven of ten of the leading causes of death, irrespective of income, race, access to care, and education.

- Time often doesn't heal the wounds linked to ACEs, but only conceals the pain.

- The earlier an ACE happens, the more difficult it is to make sense of it, especially when trusted adult support is lacking.

- We often treat the smoke, not the fire, by addressing the symptoms of disorders when we need to get at their root causes: ACEs.

- The original research was limited mostly to solidly upper-middle-class individuals—white, college educated, with good jobs and health insurance. Conditions and outcomes are often worse for high-risk groups, such as poor, urban, minority, military, and prison groups.

These statistics are alarming, yet we now know that there is much we can do to counter the effects of ACEs, once we understand the challenges we are facing. Let's begin by increasing your own ACE awareness. A copy of this worksheet is also available at http://www.newharbinger.com/46646.

What's Your ACE Score?

It's helpful to be aware of risks to your health so that you can address them with appropriate actions. For each item, check yes or no as it applies to your early life.

Prior to your eighteenth birthday:

	Yes	No
1. Did a parent or other adult in the household **often**... Swear at you, insult you, put you down, or humiliate you? **or** Act in a way that made you afraid that you might be physically hurt?		
2. Did a parent or other adult in the household **often**... Push, grab, slap, or throw something at you? **or** **Ever** hit you so hard that you had marks or were injured?		
3. Did an adult or person at least five years older than you **ever**... Touch or fondle you or have you touch their body in a sexual way? **or** Attempt or actually have oral, anal, or vaginal intercourse with you?		
4. Did you **often** feel that... No one in your family loved you or thought you were important or special? **or** Your family didn't look out for each other, feel close to each other, or support each other?		
5. Did you **often** feel that... You didn't have enough to eat, had to wear dirty clothes, and had no one to protect you? **or** Your parents were too drunk or high to take care of you or take you to the doctor if you needed it?		

	Yes	No
6. Were your parents ever divorced or separated?		
7. Was your mother or stepmother: **Often** pushed, grabbed, slapped, or had something thrown at her? **or** **Sometimes** or **often** kicked, bitten, hit with a fist, or hit with something hard? **or** **Ever** repeatedly hit over the course of at least a few minutes or threatened with a gun or knife?		
8. Did you live with anyone who was a problem drinker or an alcoholic, or who used street drugs?		
9. Was a household member depressed or mentally ill, or did a household member attempt suicide?		
10. Did a household member go to prison?		
Total the number of check marks in the "Yes" column. This is your ACE score.		

Adapted slightly from The ACE Questionnaire. Public domain.

Other ACEs

The original research linked only the ten ACEs most commonly reported by middle-class patients to undesirable health outcomes. However, many other ACEs can potentially impact health in a lasting way. Some are obvious; some are more subtle and perhaps not even consciously recalled. Preliminary data suggest that the traditional ACEs relating to household stressors seem to have greater effects on health and functioning than stressors at the community level. The scale below will expand your awareness to other ACEs that might be affecting your well-being. A copy of this worksheet is also available at http://www.newharbinger.com/46646.

Expanded ACEs Awareness Scale

Place a check mark beside any item if you experienced or witnessed it prior to your eighteenth birthday:

☐ 1. Loss of parent or guardian (due to death, murder, deportation, abduction, deployment to war zone, etc.)

☐ 2. Loss of a close family member or friend (due to death, murder, deportation, abduction, deployment to war zone, etc.)

☐ 3. Serious illness of loved one

☐ 4. Any actual or threatened household violence (any member of your household hurting or threatening to hurt another member of the household, such as mother physically abusing father)

☐ 5. Hostile parents or caregivers (who lose temper, are coercive, don't listen)

☐ 6. Parents' troubled marriage (such as parents constantly arguing)

☐ 7. Too many children to get parental attention

☐ 8. Mother's prenatal or perinatal stress

☐ 9. Anxiety about measuring up (for example, highly critical or overprotective parent[s] convey feelings of inadequacy; feeling that too much is expected of you, that you can never satisfy them; the "low whisper of inadequacy")

☐ 10. Sexual, physical, or emotional abuse by anyone (sibling or others, including date rape; being forced to see or do something sexual; seeing someone else forced to engage in sexual activity; witnessing a sibling being sexually abused)

☐ 11. Violence in the community, neighborhood, or school (such as not feeling safe in your neighborhood; seeing or hearing someone being stabbed, shot, or murdered in real life; hearing shots; being physically assaulted, mugged, or robbed; exposure to gangs or riots; your home was vandalized or burglarized; being bullied or harassed by teachers, students, or others in the community or online)

☐ 12. Discrimination (being mistreated because of disability, race, place of birth, sexual orientation, religion, and so forth)

☐ 13. Isolation, being excluded (no close friends)

☐ 14. Growing up in poverty

☐ 15. Homelessness

☐ 16. Living in a war zone

☐ 17. Witnessing gruesome injury, death, or genocide

- ☐ 18. Terrorism

- ☐ 19. Being kidnapped or abducted

- ☐ 20. Child trafficking; slavery

- ☐ 21. Forced displacement; post-migration living difficulties

- ☐ 22. Cults

- ☐ 23. Incarceration

- ☐ 24. Being forced into marriage

- ☐ 25. Natural disasters (such as floods, tornadoes, earthquakes, or hurricanes)

Research isn't yet available to show how these ACEs compound to affect your mental and physical health. However, the skills in this workbook can help lessen the suffering caused by these experiences as well.

Special Considerations for Infants and Young Children

Your experience in the womb, particularly in the third trimester, and the first three years of life are critical to your brain development, later mental health and stress reactivity, and the way you experience yourself (Lipsitt 2012). Let's take a look at adversities that can potentially wire the brain in negative ways, even without conscious recollection of the causes. Reflecting upon these considerations will help you better understand the importance of the skills you'll explore later in this workbook.

Mother's Stress

Even in the womb, the developing infant is conscious, aware of the mother's stress. This stress can be transmitted through hormones that reach the amniotic fluid, the mother's heart function, the fetus's hearing, and more. After birth, the mother who is overwhelmed or preoccupied by stress might be unable to provide the sense of safety, protection, and love that every infant needs. Interestingly, maternal dysfunction is more predictive of child pathology than even child sexual abuse (Meewisse et al. 2011). The stress experienced by your mother during or after pregnancy can contribute to your ACEs. Strains experienced by the mother include:

- The mother's physical or mental illness, including postpartum depression, drug addiction, anxiety, or recovering from surgery

- The chronic illness of another child or family member

- The mother's unresolved grief from the prior loss of an infant

- The recent death or chronic illness of another family member

- The mother was raised by traumatized parent(s)

- Marital problems (for example, the mother is preoccupied by a cheating spouse, or a partner who is emotionally or physically unsupportive)

- The pregnancy is unwanted by either parent

- The mother is preoccupied with financial worries or the fear of living in a dangerous environment (for example, with gangs or living in a war zone)

- The mother feels rejected if the baby turns away from attempts to nurse or provide affection, or the baby doesn't respond to soothing

Physical Separation from the Primary Caregiver

Another potential cause of toxic stress is separation from a primary caregiver. (Note: *Mother* and *primary caregiver* are used interchangeably, acknowledging that the mother might not always be the primary caregiver or attachment figure [Schore 2012]). Being separated as a young child from your primary caregiver can be more frightening than combat is to a soldier, leading some in adulthood to experience flashbacks when separated from others (McKenzie and Wright 1996), panic disorder (Bandelow et al. 2002), or social anxiety (Bandelow et al. 2004). Examples of separation from the primary caregiver include:

- An infant is hospitalized in an intensive care nursery or is in incubation after premature birth with little contact with the mother; the mother is anesthetized or very sick after a C-section

- An infant is taken away from the mother for circumcision

- A child is raised by hired helpers

- A child is adopted or placed in foster care, an orphanage, or a boarding school

- A child is removed from her home because of maltreatment

Prenatal or Birth Trauma

Sometimes, any of the following can register in the infant's maturing brain, contributing to ACEs:

- Obstetrical manipulations, deliberate rupture of the amniotic sac, attachment of scalp electrodes, taking scalp blood *in utero*, or other intrauterine tests (Tinnin and Gantt 2013).

- Forceps extraction, being held upside down by the heels, being placed on frigid scales, tracheal suctioning, heel lancing, premature birth, being tied or immobilized while breathing, having feeding tubes inserted, often without analgesia (Tinnin and Gantt 2013).

- Being born with the umbilical cord around the neck; a lengthy, painful, or difficult delivery, C-section, or breech birth (Heller and LaPierre 2012).

- Rectal thermometers, suppositories, or enemas (Rothschild 2000).

Serious Accident, Injury, Illness, or Medical Procedures

Another factor contributing to ACEs is accident, injury, illness, or medical procedures. Frightening surgery at a young age can be traumatic. Until 1987, surgeons routinely did infant surgery without analgesia, under the mistaken notion that infants do not feel pain. Bringing memories of childhood accidents, injury, illness, or medical procedures to conscious awareness so that they can be processed and settled can often reduce adult symptoms (Annand and Hickey 1987). The following worksheet begins to raise awareness of wounds that might need healing, the process to which we will turn throughout this workbook. A copy of this worksheet is also available at http://www.newharbinger.com/46646.

Reflect on Your Adverse Childhood Experiences

Look back on your ACE score scale, the Extended ACEs Awareness Scale, and the "Special Considerations for Infants and Young Children" section. Select three ACEs that you can remember. Write them down in the spaces provided and reflect on the experiences by answering the questions that follow without judging yourself.

Adverse Childhood Experience #1 _____

What message did this give you about yourself? How might it have influenced the way you experience yourself? Other people? The world?

_____

_____

_____

_____

How have you tried to cope with these messages?

_____

_____

_____

_____

Adverse Childhood Experience #2 _____

What message did this give you about yourself? How might it have influenced the way you experience yourself? Other people? The world?

_____

_____

_____

_____

How have you tried to cope with these messages?

_____

_____

_____

_____

Adverse Childhood Experience #3 _____

What message did this give you about yourself? How might it have influenced the way you experience yourself? Other people? The world?

_____

_____

_____

_____

How have you tried to cope with these messages?

_____

_____

_____

_____

CHAPTER 2

How ACEs Harm the Body: The Mechanisms

The mechanisms of how ACEs harm the body start with the stress response. When we are threatened or challenged, the brain prepares us for action—to fight or flee from the threat. The heart beats faster and more forcibly to move more blood to the muscles. Glucose is pumped into the blood to increase fuel for the muscles, and the airways draw in more oxygen to help the muscles burn fuel. These and many other changes are designed for movement. Ideally, the crisis passes, we've expended the energy of the stress response, and our bodies return to normal. The stress response is helpful for surviving crises in the short term.

But what if the threat is so severe or continuous that the body does not return to normal? The response that was designed to be life-saving now becomes the problem. This type of stress is what psychologists call *dysregulated stress*, and it is at the core of the ACE–health outcome relationship. Dysregulated stress— stress that is excessive or chronic—disrupts the systems of the body: hormonal, cardiovascular, immune, inflammatory, genetic, and neurological. Let's take a look at some of the ways that dysregulated stress disrupts the body's systems.

Hormonal System

Cortisol is a major stress hormone. During stress, cortisol converts the body's protein into glucose, providing energy for fight or flight, while helping to raise blood pressure. These are helpful changes in the short term because they deliver glucose, oxygen, and blood to the muscles. However, when stress is chronic, cortisol facilitates changes to keep us on high alert or prolong our ability to fight or flee. Many of these changes are unhealthy over time:

- Elevated blood pressure and blood sugar are linked to cardiovascular disease and diabetes.

- Increased fat accumulation is accompanied by cravings for sugar and fat.

- The conversion of protein into glucose suppresses immunity and impairs the development of nerve, thyroid, and lung tissue.

- Sleep is disrupted to keep us awake and on guard.

- Cognition and mood are disrupted as neural connections in key areas of the brain associated with reasoning and proper storage of memories become fewer and weaker (Harvard University n.d.). Now a vicious cycle ensues: stress destabilizes sleep, which further disrupts mood and focus.

Toxic stress also disrupts hormones that regulate your reproduction, growth, and weight. Early and prolonged exposure to cortisol is particularly disruptive to your body.

Immune System

The healthy immune system is delicately balanced, being neither over- nor underreactive. Toxic stress, however, can disrupt this delicate balance. For example, inflammation, like stress, is good in the short term—destroying pathogens and facilitating repair of damaged cells. Chronic inflammation, though, can leave your body in a constant state of alert that prevents it from ever fully recovering. Toxic stress in the early years can impair the immune system's ability to distinguish friend from foe. Later in life, the immune system might attack healthy tissue or create chronic inflammation, as seen in autoimmune disorders, allergies, asthma, and many other disorders. For example, in the brain, neuroinflammation is associated with Alzheimer's disease and depression.

Cortisol plays a key role in regulating the immune system. Too much cortisol suppresses immunity, reducing resistance to colds, flu, and other infections. If cortisol gives out from years of toxic stress, the immune system can become hyperreactive, putting us at risk for autoimmune and inflammatory disorders. It is cortisol overload in the early years that impairs the immune system's ability to distinguish friend from foe.

Genes and Epigenomes

Each of the trillions of cells in the body faithfully replicates according to an inherited genetic code contained in our DNA strands. People often assume that genes determine our susceptibility to disease. However, researchers in recent years have unearthed fascinating discoveries linking toxic stress to intracellular activities. According to their findings, only about 5 percent of diseases are determined solely by genes (Pelletier 2019). The other disorders reflect an interplay between genes and epigenomes, with epigenomes playing the greater role. Epigenomes sit alongside the DNA strands. The epigenome is like the dimmer switch on a light—turning genes on or off and regulating their activity level. Epigenomes, then, play a major role in shaping how the brain and body develop.

Toxic stress in the early years affects the epigenome, which in turn shapes brain development. The brain becomes wired to maintain high alert and to overreact to stress. The brain also becomes less able to regulate emotions, putting us at risk for mental disorders. Once altered by toxic stress, the epigenome can influence gene expression throughout life, and might even be passed down intergenerationally, putting future generations at risk for stress-related conditions.

The good news is that the epigenome is malleable. Just as toxic stress can change the epigenome for the worse, you can alter the epigenome to your advantage—often fairly rapidly—through the strategies we'll discuss later in the workbook.

Telomeres

Telomeres are DNA molecules at the tip of chromosomes strands. Just as the plastic tips on shoelaces protect the shoelaces from unraveling, telomeres protect the DNA strand from damage and ensure proper cell replication. Longer telomeres provide greater protection against cell death, inflammation, oxidative stress, and premature aging.

Telomeres shorten with accumulated stress and aging. Stress can be tripped by ACEs and the perception of threat, inadequacy, and defeat. Smoking, drinking, and lack of exercise are among other stressors that can shorten telomeres (Ridout, Khan, and Ridout 2018). Shorter telomeres change the developing brain, resulting in silencing of genes that oversee regulation of cortisol, reductions in the brain region that regulates executive function, and breakdown of neural connections between regions that regulate stress and inflammation.

Telomeres can be preserved or lengthened by boosting the enzyme telomerase. Fortunately, activities that favorably change the epigenome—including exercising, meditating, and cultivating compassion and joy—also increase telomerase levels. We'll be addressing these in this workbook as well.

Neurological System

The last trimester of pregnancy through the first three years of life are critical for brain development. During the brain's growth spurt, the child's brain is forming more than one million neural connections per second (Thompson 2018). To a great degree, the shaping of our brains by ACEs in these early years will influence our emotional well-being in the years to come.

The left side of the brain enables us to do what we value at work and school—reason, verbalize, and consciously recall dry facts. The left brain is not fully online, however, until around year three, so we might not fully remember or consciously recall memories from the earliest years or be able to put them into words.

Much of what allows us to regulate stress and emotions and thrive in relationships plays out in the right brain. The right brain is mostly online during the first two years, is dominant for the first three years, and continues to be dominant beyond the third year for emotional processes, including the nonconscious aspects of emotional processing.

In addition to regulating stress and emotions, the right brain is responsible for processing and storing the cues listed below. Notice that much of this is nonverbal and below the level of conscious awareness, especially as it relates to imprints from the earliest years.

- Nonverbal communication, including images, facial expressions, and gestures (Schore 2009; van der Kolk 2014).

- Senses, including sound, touch, pressure, sight, smell, taste, pain, and vibrations.

- Awareness of bodily states and their connection to emotions—for example, how the heart or gut is experiencing emotional arousal (Schore 2012; van der Kolk 2014).

- Survival tendencies. Toxic stress, for example, might ingrain the tendency to run, fight, freeze, hunch the shoulders, or tighten the gut when stressed (Ogden and Fisher 2015).

- Self-awareness, the basic sense of self, and implicit memory (discussed below). To a great degree, self-esteem is imprinted as a felt sense in the right brain by the first three years, and stored *implicitly* below conscious awareness (Wilkinson 2010). Such imprints are usually not responsive to logic or words.

Later on, we'll address how imprints from the early years can be rewired, not through logic and words, but through strategies involving imagery, emotions, and body-based skills.

What Is Implicit Memory?

Understanding implicit memory helps to complete our understanding of the neurological system. The left brain processes and stores *explicit* memories—those that can be consciously recalled and described with words, dry details, and appropriate emotions. The right brain processes and stores *implicit* memories. These memories are nonverbal and are stored below the level of conscious awareness. They have a strong feeling tone and a felt sense. One might sense a deep, pervasive perception—a nameless dread, the feeling that one is not good enough, the sense that something is terribly wrong, the sense of being on edge, or self-loathing. One might experience this emotionally or deep in the body without being able to put the feeling into words or understand where it comes from. There might be an impulse to flee or hide. As you'll see in the next chapter, this felt sense might be ingrained in the first three years of life in the right brain as a result of ACEs. A memory of being mistreated might be locked in with all the original emotions, sensations, images, and visceral feelings. The feelings might be helplessness, rage, anxiety, or shame—and it feels like that is who you are (Wilkinson 2010). All these buried aspects of memory can be triggered by present events, which stir up the same emotions, sensations, and wordless felt sense. We'll discuss this further in chapter 3, which explains the psychology of ACEs.

Implicit memories can form at any age as the result of overwhelming stress. They can be imprinted especially in the earliest years before the left brain matures. (The earlier that one experiences ACEs, the more likely the memories will be stored as implicit memories.) Through epigenetic influences, ACEs can impair the development of key brain regions that are responsible for regulating stress and emotions, storing memories with appropriate emotions, and transmitting memories to areas that can consciously recall and verbalize them.

Implicit memories can also be formed in later years when toxic stress takes key brain areas responsible for verbalizing, reasoning, calming, and feeling whole off-line. In dire circumstances, the brain is concerned only that you fight or flee to safety. The other functions mentioned are not critical for immediate survival.

Although explicit memories tend to fade with age, implicit memories do not (Lewis, Amini, and Lannon 2000). As mentioned, once implicit memories are formed, they may be triggered by present events. Because these memories are not managed by the logical mind, they resurface with the same emotions and sensations as when originally experienced. Thus, your boss's criticism might feel just like being severely scolded as a child by a critical parent. Never mind that the adult being criticized is now "successful." Because implicit memories are not settled and situated in the verbal and logical brain, they are only marginally affected by words or logic. Other approaches are called for, as we'll soon see. These approaches do not target primarily the logical, verbal left brain, but the regions of the brain that regulate emotions, images, and bodily sensations.

You can begin to manage implicit memories by noticing how you experience them—in a calm, accepting, nonjudgmental way. The exercise below will help you do this. A copy of this worksheet is also available at http://www.newharbinger.com/46646.

How Do You Experience Implicit Memories?

Are there times you struggle with unpleasant feelings, sensations, thoughts, or behaviors and, perhaps, you're not sure why? Without passing judgment as to whether this is good or bad, just notice this with curious interest. Write about this. What do you experience? When? Where specifically in your body do you sense this?

_____

_____

_____

_____

_____

_____

Imagine that you wake up tomorrow feeling different, in a pleasant way. What might that feel like? Where would you feel that in your body?

_____

_____

_____

_____

_____

_____

_____

_____

_____

_____

CHAPTER 3

How ACEs Shape Psychology

In front of me in the checkout line on a recent trip to the grocery store were a mother and her four children. With pleasant efficiency, the older children were helping their mother with the scanning. Occasionally, they would give a smile and soothing word to the two younger children sitting in the cart. The children seemed to radiate a secure sense of themselves and a quiet, inner gladness. They seemed connected to each other and to their mother, who comfortably interacted with them. One of the older children noticed me smiling at the scene and smiled back with her eyes. And I thought, "How fortunate those children are to be so securely attached."

Attachment—whether secure or insecure—plays a critical role in the development of our sense of self and the way our brain functions. As you'll see shortly, secure attachment strengthens individuals in various ways, while ACEs often lead to attachment disruptions that can damage growing children in many ways. Let's look first at secure attachment.

Secure Attachment

Attachment reflects a normal, beautiful, innate desire to bond lovingly with parent(s) or caregivers. While attachment figures can be a father, grandparents, siblings, or others, most infants prefer the mother for comfort when distressed, and function best with two secure caregiver relationships (Cassidy 2008).* *Secure* attachment reflects the deep emotional bond that forms in the first months of life between an infant and the primary caregiver when the child feels consistently loved and cared for. The caregiver conveys in many ways that the child is safe, protected, and valued: by holding, skin-to-skin touching, kissing, and hugging; by loving gazes and facial expressions; by safe, rhythmic gestures and vocal sounds; by timely attention to the infant's needs; and by smiling, laughing, and having fun with the child. Through repeated encounters that are sensitive to the child's needs, the child learns that the caregiver is available and responsive, and will not abandon her.

---

* *Note:* Recognizing various arrangements, and following the practice of neuropsychologist and attachment researcher Allan Schore (2012), the terms "mother" and "primary caregiver" will be used interchangeably throughout this workbook. The terms "parent(s)," "primary caregiver(s)," and "father(s)" will also be used interchangeably.

What results is a felt sense, rather than one that is recalled. Secure attachment is imprinted in the infant's sensing and emotional right hemisphere in the first months of life and tends to operate for life (Schore 2009). These imprints are formed in the earliest months of life, before the verbal and logical areas of the left brain develop. Although they don't understand words, newborns sense and imprint nonverbal messages.

The infant who is securely attached to an attuned parent internalizes the messages—more sensed than reasoned—"I am loved just as I am, I matter, and I have worth because the people who created me value me." The baby forms an impression of what love feels like long before memories of events develop. And the growing child will love himself in the same way as the mother did (Lewis, Amini, and Lannon 2000).

Secure attachment changes the brain in favorable ways, predicting in later years:

- Better self-esteem and a strong sense of self (for example, Brisch 2011; Karen 1994; Schore 2012; Wilkinson 2010).

- Better mental and physical health (McEwen 2017). For example, secure attachment protects against PTSD (Allen, Coyne, and Huntoon 1998).

- Greater awareness of, and connection to, one's emotions and body (Schore 2012).

- Greater resilience and confidence (Mikulincer and Shaver 2008).

- Better ability to tolerate and regulate distress. The infant internalizes the mother's calmness, resulting in a more serene nervous system. From the soothing mother, the child learns to self-soothe. When the mother returns reasonably quickly to the distressed infant, the developing child learns not to overreact because "disruptions will be set right" (Schore 2012, 236).

- Greater ability to trust and connect with other people. Others and the world are viewed as safe and predictable, consistent with early experiences with the primary caregiver(s) (Snyder and Lopez 2007).

- A greater likelihood of viewing God as loving (Granqvist et al. 2007).

In short, loving bonds formed in the earliest years profoundly benefit the adult. This is why Siegel has repeated, "To grow a child's mind, nurture a baby's heart" (1999, 189). But what happens when the child does not experience these loving bonds?

Insecure Attachment

ACEs can disrupt the development of healthy child–caregiver bonds. This disruption often results in insecure attachment, the frightening feeling of being unloved. The inner wounds caused by attachment disruptions are typically ingrained in the early months of life (Siegel 1999). When the infant is highly stressed by attachment disruptions, two changes occur: 1) the brain becomes wired to remain on high alert and 2) one's healthy sense of self is damaged. Here's how this happens.

Severe early childhood trauma creates a child with equally intense coping mechanisms— these children are often seen as "mature for their age" and "old souls." While maybe true, it often negates the fact that their innocence was taken away at an early age and they are in survival mode.

—Azia Archer

The highly stressed mother—who perhaps is preoccupied, neglectful, traumatized, rejecting, or abusive—does not fully connect with the infant in a loving way. This is stressful to the infant, who responds by secreting more cortisol. Cortisol epigenetically influences the early developing right brain, with its deep connections to the nerves that sense and regulate the body (Schore 1997, 2012). Harmful changes occur in regions that regulate one's emotions, stress arousal (Shariful and Nemeroff 2017), and sense of self (Goddard 2017). These alterations, which are consistent with those seen in anxiety and PTSD (McEwen 2017), shape the way we later react to stress, as well as the way we experience ourselves. All this plays out in the background, beneath conscious awareness.

Notice that a damaged sense of self resulting from attachment disruptions can be imprinted implicitly in the nonverbal right brain, typically by the eighteenth month of life. For example, the infant might internalize the caregiver's disgusted look or angry tone of voice. This is stored in the right brain, perhaps as a troubling image, an unpleasant internal bodily state, a distressing emotion, wordless self-dislike, or a survival impulse to tense up under stress. Because the sense of self that is damaged by early toxic stress is not situated in the verbal, logical left brain, words and logic alone typically do not effectively change it (Wilkinson 2010).

There is cause for hope, though. Secure attachment tends to persist throughout life, even through difficult circumstances, while insecure attachment is malleable, able to be changed to a more secure style (Berlin, Cassidy, and Appleyard 2008). Attachment style change starts with kind, nonjudgmental awareness, so please start by rating yourself on the "Effects of Insecure Attachment Scale" on the following pages. A copy of this worksheet is also available at http://www.newharbinger.com/46646.

Effects of Insecure Attachment Scale

People vary in how they respond to attachment disruptions. Insecure attachment in childhood can result in many different adult patterns. Again, many of these symptoms might play out in the background, below conscious awareness. To raise awareness of how insecure attachment might be playing out in your present life, please check the items below that describe you. Just notice what comes up with curious interest and without judging.

Your Emotional and Physical Arousal

I experience…

- ☐ Difficulty regulating emotions—anxiety, including panic attacks, separation anxiety, abandonment fear, and social anxiety; depression; anger; feeling overwhelmed, helpless, or fearful; can't tolerate being alone; difficulty experiencing positive emotions

- ☐ High stress arousal—on edge, easily startled, trouble concentrating or sleeping, irritability, can't be calmed. Or numb, collapsed, shut down, flat.

How You Experience Yourself

ACEs can negatively affect your basic sense of self—your identity at the core—in ways that appear on brain scans, according to neuroscientist Ruth Lanius (in Nakazawa 2015), and might manifest as:

- ☐ Low self-esteem (feeling defective, inadequate, not good enough, unlovable, powerless, helpless)

- ☐ Shame, self-loathing, self-contempt

- ☐ Feeling emptiness, nothingness, little sense of self

- ☐ Feeling that you are not normal

- ☐ Feeling dead inside

- ☐ Feeling isolated, alienated, alone; rejected, disconnected from others; you don't belong, you are not "at home"

- ☐ Lacking confidence in relationships; feeling unworthy or not good enough

Your Worldview

I think that…

- ☐ *The world isn't safe.*

- ☐ *I don't really belong anywhere.*

- ☐ *Authority figures are frightening or uncomfortable.*

- ☐ *Relationships are scary.*

- ☐ *People are not to be trusted or counted on.*

Your Coping Methods

I...

- ☐ Am hypersensitive to criticism or rejection.

- ☐ Present a facade of calm that is shaken under intense distress.

- ☐ Present a facade of success (I look successful and confident on the outside, while feeling like a mess inside).

- ☐ Use extreme, inflexible defenses—self-protecting, keeping others away, extreme independence; or letting too many people in (weak boundaries); extreme dependence.

- ☐ Am typically dissatisfied with myself or others.

- ☐ Compensate for a feeling of inadequacy by:

  - ☐ Narcissism—a facade of superiority that masks vulnerability.

  - ☐ Hiding to protect myself—becoming invisible like a shrinking violet; withdrawing from people.

  - ☐ Being harshly critical of self or others.

  - ☐ Demanding others' attention (attention that I didn't receive early in life).

  - ☐ Perfectionism, overachievement (immoderate pursuit of wealth, being highly competitive, obsessing over one's body image through excessive dieting, body sculpting, etc.).

  - ☐ Pleasing behavior.

  - ☐ Avoiding problems or challenges; giving up (fearing that one might fail and disappoint self or others).

- ☐ Have trouble empathizing (empathy wasn't modeled in the early years).

- ☐ Can't tolerate negative or even positive emotions; am numbing emotions, hiding my feelings for fear that others won't accept or acknowledge them.

- ☐ Find it difficult to express emotions with words; instead, emotions are expressed through physical symptoms, such as asthma, diarrhea, infections, skin conditions, pain, collapsing, etc.

- ☐ Am overly emotional—overreacting or becoming dramatic when encountering frustration, disappointments, being ignored, being criticized, etc.

- ☐ Suppress or ignore painful feelings; am unaware of feelings; am overly cerebral or intellectual; deny or avoid unpleasant feelings.

- ☐ Have difficulty connecting or cooperating with others.

☐ Self-medicate emotional pain with substances (drugs seem more dependable than people).

☐ Harm myself, or risk harm to myself, through drugs, self-injury, casual sex, or other risky behaviors or addictions (Lewis, Amini, and Lannon 2000, note that opioids extinguish physical pain, but also the emotional pain from separation or ending a relationship. Self-harm releases opiates. So cutting, for example, now makes sense for at least one reason—the hunger for love. They add [94] that "warm human contact also generates internal opiate release.").

Your Posture
If other people were looking at me, they'd likely think that my posture is...

☐ Rigid (self-protecting).

☐ Slumped (often seen in people who learned that caregivers won't respond).

Spoken or Unspoken Messages
Faulty nurturing in the early years can ingrain messages that are often more felt than thought. As you've matured, these feelings might be expressed in words or unspoken thoughts:

☐ Something is wrong with me.

☐ My basic, core self is deeply and permanently damaged.

☐ I don't matter.

☐ I'm no good, empty.

☐ I was treated like trash, so I must be trash.

☐ I don't belong.

☐ I displeased my caregiver; therefore, I am unlovable.

☐ I'm bad.

☐ I'm powerless, helpless.

☐ I'm inferior as a person to others.

☐ I'm defective, worthless.

☐ The world is dangerous. Something bad is about to happen. Stay on alert (wordless dread).

☐ My feelings don't matter; no one cares what I feel.

☐ It's uncomfortable to be around people.

☐ I must be perfect to be loved.

☐ I'm not enough; I should be more.

☐ If I'm not perfect, then I'm a loser.

Your Trauma Symptoms

I experience…

☐ Nightmares, flashbacks, or other intrusive memories. (Typically these are nonverbal, visual, and experienced in the body. These signal that a memory is unprocessed or unsettled.)

☐ A shutdown on my loving, happy nature, instead being hypervigilant, easily startled, irritable, or hyperactive.

☐ State-dependent stress. Stress, or reminders of the stressful past, pull up either implicit or explicit memories, along with the original emotions, sensations, survival impulses, and visceral responses (such as in the gut, heart, chest, throat, or lungs). Thus, being ignored by a significant other might trigger the feeling of being neglected by one's caregiver in the early years. Or, a visit home might trigger feelings of inadequacy.

☐ Dissociation—feeling that you or the world around you is unreal; feeling that you are drifting away from your body or the present when things are stressful.

☐ Numbness.

☐ Blank stare; "thousand-yard stare."

☐ Bouncing between extremes ("I'm on top of the world or I'm down in the dumps," "My loved one is an angel or [when he/she disappoints] despicable.").

Based on Brisch 2011; Heller and LaPierre 2012; Hendel 2018; Mellin 2010; Schore 2012; Siegel 1999; Steele 2007; Takikawa 2004; and van der Kolk 2014.

Making Sense of the Effects of Insecure Attachment Scale

It can be reassuring to realize that your reactions make sense. They are common, understandable responses to attachment disruptions. You are not alone. Many others have experienced similar reactions in response to attachment disruptions. Later on in this workbook, you'll learn ways to bring compassion to these reactions and soften their impact. You'll also learn to compensate for your caregiver's shortcomings in filling your attachment needs. To help you in this process, let's explore what effective caregivers provide and how they do so.

The Power of Healthy Caregiving

This section will help you better understand the important roles that caregivers play in creating secure attachment. This understanding will help you appreciate the reasons for a number of the skills you'll practice later in this workbook. We'll be focusing specifically on the research on the importance of mothers and fathers, because nearly all the research to date has focused on children's attachment bonds to parents. Please keep in mind, though, that sustained, positive relationships with other caring, genuinely interested adults can be instrumental in filling attachment needs. Please also remember that if your caregivers did not effectively meet your attachment needs, it is especially important that you learn to become a good parent to yourself. Here's what we know from the research about a baby's secure attachment bond with the mother and father.

Takikawa (2004) observed that babies have consciousness from the beginning, knowing if they are wanted and loved. They are born looking for us, locking on the mother's face, wanting to cuddle—and we respond. At nursing distance, six to twelve inches, a soul-to-soul connection is formed between baby and mother, a sacred melting together. The child has a natural impulse to nurse with peace and quiet, to feel the warmth of the mother's skin, the comfort of parents' arms. Cared for in this way, the child's need to feel honored, welcomed, needed, and known by the caregiver(s) is met.

Most attachment research has studied the mother–infant relationship. The critical importance of this relationship is well documented. The mother–infant bond forms in the first year (Schore 2012). During the earliest months of life, the infant usually prefers to turn to the mother for comfort. However, research indicates that the best-functioning children have two secure attachment relationships and that mothers and fathers can affect children in complementary ways (Cassidy 2008). Whereas the mother's influence is critically important from the beginning, stable, loving fathers uniquely and increasingly contribute from the beginning and as the child matures (Grossman et al. 2008). For example, the more the father visits the hospital to see a premature infant, the more quickly the infant leaves the hospital (Levy-Shiff et al. 1990).

The baby's left brain, including speech centers, begins a growth spurt in the second year of life. During this time, the baby begins to interact more with the father, who tends to impact the left brain over and above the ways mothers do (Schore 2012). For example, when fathers read to children in the early months, the children use more advanced language at age three (Raeburn 2015). The father's absence in the second year can be more detrimental than absence in the first year of life (Schore 2012). Involved, loving fathers can also:

- Promote the development of inner security and self-esteem by providing love and approval (Michigan DHHS 2017). Kendrick and Kendrick (2011) note that children who didn't get their father's approval can spend the rest of their lives trying to win others' approval.

- Contribute indirectly to the child's attachment security by helping mothers be happy so they can more effectively mother.

- Help children grow greater resilience and higher IQ, while reducing the risk of mental illness, drug use, suicide, school failure, behavioral disorders, and crime (Michigan DHHS 2017; Farrell and Gray 2018; Popenoe 1996; Zinsmeister 1992). Boys seem to do particularly poorly in broken families where fathers are absent (Farrell and Gray 2018).

- Help instill a moral compass, boundaries, behavioral control, self-respect, responsibility, a sense of adventure, a sense of service, empathy, and appreciation of one's sexual identity (Farrell and Gray 2018; Zinsmeister 1992).

- Teach children how to play, compete, and restrain aggression. For example, in roughhousing with a caring father, children can learn what is safe and what is not appropriate (Farrell and Gray 2018; Popence 1996; Schore 2012).

- Push children a little and challenge them, resulting in confidence as they learn to explore and overcome danger (mothers tend to keep kids safe); (Grossman et al. 2008).

- Provide spiritual support and modeling. For example, if the father regularly attends religious services, the children are ten to twenty times more likely to do so when they're adults, compared to when the father does not attend—irrespective of the mother's attendance patterns (Haug and Wanner 2000).

- Help daughters develop a wholesome view of sexuality and their own femininity, heterosexual trust, and the ability to relate to men (Popence 1996). Daughters raised with a father's love are more likely to feel worthy of love, and less likely to seek love in unhealthy ways (Farrell and Gray 2018; Zinsmeister 1992).

Reprinted with permission of Megan Warren, Starry Night Art Studio, Fullerton, CA. © 2018 Megan Warren.

So it is clear that both primary caregivers ideally make important contributions to the growing child's development. Yet many fathers today are increasingly absent from parenting—perhaps through divorce or by being preoccupied with work, entertainment, recreation, or their own ACEs. Fathers can also be absent due to mental illness, just as the mothers can be. For example, 10 percent of fathers experience postpartum depression (Raeburn 2014).

For a variety of reasons, fathers sometimes fail to recognize how important their parenting contributions are to the child's development. For example, if fathers are present at birth, they tend to bond more with their children. If fathers are absent during pregnancy, infants are more likely to be born prematurely or with lower birth weight (see Raeburn 2014). The loss of a father during pregnancy even increases the risk of schizophrenia (Huttunen and Niskanen 1978).

If you didn't have loving, involved parents in your early years, take heart. Imagery exercises that you'll practice shortly can help you experience the love that ideal parents would have provided, rewiring your brain as though you had actually experienced that nurturing.

Three Final Aspects of ACEs Psychology

Let's round out your understanding of the psychology of ACEs by exploring three important topics: inner security, ACEs occurring after the earliest years, and shame. These topics complete the foundations for the skills you will practice later on.

Inner Security

To feel secure in an unpredictable world is a precious gift. The diction-ary defines "security" as tranquility and freedom from fear, doubt, and undue concern about others' judgments. It is a sense of safety, certainty, or confidence, and not being unduly endangered by threats. It is feeling firm, strong, stable, anchored, and not likely to give way.

> *I still close my eyes and go home—I can always draw from that.*
>
> —Dolly Parton

We can have *outward* security against *external* threats by acquiring skills, experience, and resources. Examples of this type of outward security include:

- Financial security—having enough money (think Social Security)

- Physical security—living in a safe home and community, being able to protect yourself or call on others to do so

- Relationship security—members are committed to stay and nurture one another

- Job security—feeling confident of your employment and education

These forms of security are important and worthy of pursuit. However, due to the unpredictable nature of the world, external securities can never be 100 percent certain. In this workbook, we are focusing on *internal*, emotional security. This is the inner security that keeps us going when things get difficult; it is the only form that we can really always depend on. Inner security is harder to define because you can't see it, but it feels like the following:

- A sense of calm; feeling settled, not in turmoil; inner peace even if the world is in chaos

- Being anchored in self-worth that is not shaken by external events, such as the rise and fall of the stock market

- Being self-accepting—appreciating yourself, despite faults

- Being glad to be who you are—you can look in the mirror with inner delight, affection, and self-respect, not self-doubt or shame

- Being comfortable with life's inevitable challenges—not unduly worried; confident that you can cope with most things reasonably well

- Feeling safe with others' judgments—after all, they are just imperfect people, too

- Knowing that there is more to you than your missteps and faults—or the way others treat you

It is natural to feel insecure and inadequate at times, or even often. We all feel that way at times. This is part of being mortal. But it is possible to feel more and more inwardly secure as we develop new skills and resources.

Inner security in the midst of chaos can be acquired from your family of origin, later loving relationships, spiritual resources, and the acquisition of key coping skills. If you weren't fortunate enough to have loving bonds and secure attachment experiences in childhood, you can learn to become a good parent to yourself and meet the unmet needs of the earlier years. These are important aims of this workbook.

What About ACEs Occurring After the Earliest Years?

The effects of ACEs can pile on after the earliest years. By the third and fourth years of life, both sides of the brain are "online"—sufficiently developed and functional. Once both sides of a child's brain are online, further effects of ACEs, such as low self-esteem and shame, can be ingrained either implicitly or explicitly (Siegel 1999). For example, living with a parent who is harshly critical can explicitly imprint or reinforce already low self-esteem.

Shame

Have you known people who are intelligent, pleasant, attractive, and even successful in the world's eyes, yet who intensely dislike themselves? Shame helps to explain this. Shame is closely related to insecure attachment and low self-esteem, both effects of ACEs.

First, some clarification. Shame differs from guilt. The logical mind accepts appropriate guilt, which acknowledges that we've done something wrong and motivates us to take appropriate corrective action. However, the logical mind is not fully developed in the early years. And in the later years of childhood, toxic stress can take the logical mind off-line because the brain is not concerned with logic when survival is at stake. This opens the door for shame to take root. Shame is a sense of feeling bad to the core—self-loathing or self-contempt. Shame can be imprinted implicitly in the right brain as a felt sense—emotions and bodily perceptions—as a result of repeated attachment disruptions occurring within the first eighteen months of life (Schore 1994, 2003). For example, an infant might internalize an abusive or neglectful caregiver's nonverbal messages that convey that the infant is not valued and does not matter. While realistic guilt can promote well-being, shame does not. Shame is part of your felt sense that plays out in many ways that overlap with insecure attachment, as shown in appendix B. We'll return to this important topic in later chapters.

Shame ingrained in the early years is typically resistant to external successes, such as career or educational achievements: no matter how successful you are, that persistent sense of shame can lurk within. Nor does it typically respond to verbal persuasion—attempts by you or others to talk you out of it. Healing shame is more about the heart. As you'll soon see, shame is changed by holding it with acceptance, understanding, and compassion—and rewiring its associated neural pathways. You'll soon learn the skills to do just that in this workbook.

What Have You Learned So Far?

The research is clear: childhood adversity, attachment disruption, and the resulting loss of self-esteem can shape your psychology and affect your health decades later (for example, Slobodin et al. 2011; review in Price, Connor, and Allen 2017). Now you know why. Brisch (2011, 284) has summarized the attachment research well: "Attachment processes represent a challenge that may begin before birth—perhaps even before conception—and endure into old age." And later childhood adversities can pile on attachment disruptions.

It's helpful to see what you are up against; it's even more helpful to know how to break the links between ACEs and unhealthy outcomes. You can learn to rewire your brain so that it becomes more resilient to stress.

Perspective-taking helps. Experiencing childhood adversity is not all bad. ACEs can spur us to grow stronger, to learn new skills that we lacked back then. In fact, some research even suggests that those with an ACE score of zero who don't acquire resilience can have a higher risk for inflammation and depression later in life than those who have been seasoned by some adversity (see Nakazawa 2015; Young-Wolff et al. 2019). I've had the privilege of interviewing people who have survived enormous hardship. They often say that they wouldn't have chosen the experiences they endured, but now, looking back, they wouldn't trade them for any amount of money. Even your unpleasant experience can be turned to your advantage.

In future chapters, you will build on the foundational understanding that you've gained so far to develop skills and strategies to heal and become more resilient. You are more fortunate than your ancestors, who perhaps repeated harmful familial patterns and did not know what you will learn. You can understand what made them and your caregivers tick. You can determine to be a transition person in your family tree, breaking the cycle of suffering. Even now, you can discover your strengths and use your experience to heal and become stronger. If your hurdles in life have been higher than others', you will likely have to work at it. It may take longer, but the promise of progression is certain. You might think of this workbook as caring for the soul—the core of who you are. That core remains intact and capable of progressing, despite the way you may have been treated and despite what you have experienced in the past.

Constructive change is far more likely to occur when we understand with the heart. Before moving on, complete the following exercise to gain perspective on your early years. A copy of this worksheet is also available at http://www.newharbinger.com/46646.

Remembering My Family

Ponder the following questions and respond in writing. Without judging, just notice what comes up. Take your time. Being able to sit with your responses with equanimity—and kind acceptance of what you experienced—is an important step in the healing process.

1. In your early years, where did you live? Who lived with you?

_____

_____

_____

_____

2. Did people in your home enjoy each other's company?

_____

_____

_____

_____

3. How did adults in your home resolve their disagreements?

_____

_____

_____

_____

4. Did anyone in your early years make you feel special? Safe?

_____

_____

_____

_____

_____

5. Who was (were) your primary caregiver(s) in your early years?

_____

_____

_____

_____

_____

6. How would you describe them? Can you think of several strengths and weaknesses that describe them?

_____

_____

_____

_____

_____

7. How would you describe your relationship with each of them?

_____

_____

_____

_____

_____

8. How did they discipline you?

_____

_____

_____

_____

9. When you were little, what did you do when you were upset? Who did you turn to for comfort? What would happen?

_____

_____

_____

_____

_____

10. Can you describe the first time you were separated from your parent(s)? What was that like for you? How did they respond?

_____

_____

_____

_____

_____

11. Did you ever feel rejected as a child by your parent(s)? If so, what was that like for you?

_____

_____

_____

_____

_____

12. What was most difficult for you regarding your early years?

_____

_____

_____

_____

_____

13. How have your early childhood experiences affected you today for good and bad?

_____

_____

_____

_____

_____

14. What other family members or caregivers influenced you for good and bad?

_____

_____

_____

_____

_____

15. Who or what has helped you survive so far? What inner strengths, interests, and motivations got you through? What resources around you have supported you?

_____

_____

_____

_____

_____

Adapted from George, Kaplan, and Main 1985; van der Kolk 2015a.

PART II

Solutions

About Healing

CHAPTER 4

The Promise of Healing

Anyone can be overwhelmed and wounded by toxic stress, especially in the earlier years before coping skills are learned and the brain fully develops—and especially without a protective caregiver. However, there is very good reason for hope. Every pain or hurt resulting from toxic stress can be substantially lessened, even decades later. The brain is plastic; it can be rewired. Hidden wounds can heal if we have the courage to address them with understanding, compassion, and skill. All solutions seem to regulate the stress response, favorably alter the epigenome, and preserve telomeres. In addition, the solutions rewire harmful ACE programming in the brain to change the way we experience ourselves.

What heals the traumatized brain? A guiding principle is that mature love, not time, is the healing agent! Love—sometimes called by its other names, such as caring, respect, acceptance, compassion, loving-kindness, gentle friendliness, or concern—changes the brain and body in beneficial ways. Love softens traumatic memories. And memories of being loved that we *access or create* help us tolerate suffering. As one of the world's foremost neuroscientists Richard Davidson (2009) remarked regarding love's capacity to reshape the brain, "It all comes down to love." If love was in short supply in the developing years, you can learn to supply it later in life.

In addition, a major therapeutic goal is to cause your body and right brain, where trauma is lodged, to feel safe and calm. Along with experiencing mature love, experiencing safety and calm create the condition where trauma memories can rewire and settle (van der Kolk 2015b). Perception also matters. Those who view suffering as awful and irreversibly wounding fare more poorly than those who view suffering as a challenging experience that calls us to acquire new inner strengths and coping skills. Lastly, *resilience* refers to the inner strengths and coping skills found in effective copers. Resilience helps people prevent and recover from stress-related conditions, while optimizing well-being and functioning. To a great degree, you can grow resilience. If those who went before you lacked resilience and the know-how to cope with toxic stress, you can become the transition person in your family.

Opening Up

We are indeed as sick as our secrets. It is not healthy to keep painful secrets bottled up inside. The road to healing and resilience-building starts with awareness. It is therapeutic to simply understand what is causing your pain and why, as you can appreciate by now. And having a constructive outlet for painful secrets furthers the healing journey. Most people find it somewhat curative to simply talk about ACEs with a caring person. Many health professionals now advocate routine screening for ACEs as part of medical intakes, just as we assess weight and blood pressure. In a large study, doctors asked patients to tell them how the ACEs that they'd reported on a screening tool had impacted them later in life. The patients said they felt accepted as doctors really listened to their deepest secrets and still wanted to see them again. Their stress of secret-keeping was reduced. Screening for ACEs in this way resulted in a 35 percent drop in doctor visits and an 11 percent drop in emergency room visits. You might also wish to discuss with your doctor the possibility of seeing a psychotherapist who has experience with resolving troubling memories related to ACEs.

Healing Attitudes

Give yourself credit for being resilient enough to survive your adverse experiences thus far, for surviving a difficult childhood. Appreciate that it has taken important inner strengths to do so. Know that you are already starting with inner strengths that can be grown.

Resolve to create a happier childhood by healing and creating joy. Determine to heal your emotional wounds, including traumatic wounds. Trauma is an experience that overwhelms your coping abilities at the time. There is no shame in being traumatized. Anyone can be overwhelmed, but anyone can also learn to recover. The first step is to heal the hidden wounds so that you can move ahead unburdened. Think of trying to walk through the woods with a broken ankle. The pain distracts you from enjoying nature's beauty. So it's wise to take the time needed to heal before undertaking such an endeavor. Similarly, it is wise to heal hidden emotional wounds so that you can enjoy your journey through life. Because trauma is by nature overwhelming, it might be useful to enlist the help of a trauma specialist. An effective trauma therapist understands that words and logic alone rarely go deep enough to heal memories of toxic childhood stress, which are not stored in the verbal and logical parts of the brain. Treating trauma requires specially trained psychotherapists. Finding such a therapist can go a long way toward reducing needless, prolonged suffering.

Trauma Basics

Think of something mildly unpleasant that you experienced within the last week. You can probably readily recall the details of what happened. The memory has a beginning, a middle, and an end. Like a file in a filing cabinet, you can take the memory out and look at it with appropriate emotion. You can remember when the memory occurred, and you can remember the event in context with other memories. For instance, say you were in a hurry last week and couldn't find your misplaced car keys. Although it was frustrating, you can remember other times when you were organized and realize that this was an isolated occurrence. So you can file away the memory without undue stress.

Now consider a traumatic memory, such as abuse. When undergoing toxic stress, the parts of the brain that store memories in a cool, logical way—like files in a filing cabinet—are either undeveloped or go offline (recall that during extreme stress, survival trumps logic). The traumatic memory is now stored "on the desktop," like the only memory on file—keeping us on high alert even though the danger has passed.

The traumatic memory is highly emotionally charged because strong emotions during survival mode are necessary to push us to fight or flee danger. Thoughts such as "I'm helpless" or "No one will love me if I don't appear normal" are usually embedded in the memory below conscious awareness—more as a felt sense because the thinking areas of the brain either shut down or were not yet developed. This is part of the brain's helpful hardwiring: we don't want to overthink when survival demands immediate action.

Fragments of the memory are not integrated—they do not hold together. Therefore, when the traumatic memory is triggered by a reminder of the event, only some of the memory fragments typically come to awareness. So when shopping, you might get a whiff of a certain cologne. You become nauseous without realizing why. That cologne reminds you of being mistreated by a man who wore that cologne. Perhaps you also feel anxious without realizing why. The brain normally stores memories that are important to survival without changing them. When triggered, these memories cause us to react the same way, even though this survival response is no longer needed. As long as we avoid the original memory and do not process or settle it, the original memory is liable to be triggered. Perhaps only a feeling of stress triggers a stressful memory such that parts of the memory resurface. This is called *state-dependent* memory.

The principle for healing traumatic memories is *reconsolidation*. This principle states that memories are malleable. That is, when we bring the various aspects of a toxic memory to conscious awareness, the brain has a chance to change the memory. Thus, if you were to recall the bodily sensations, emotions, thoughts, and images of a traumatic memory and relate the details to someone who witnesses your story with respect, then respect begins to replace shame. If you can calm yourself during the retelling of the traumatic memory, then calmness begins to replace the arousal that has been tied to the memory. If you can imagine a different outcome to the traumatic memory, then the new image begins to replace the old one.

Most effective trauma treatments rely on the principle of reconsolidation. Recall that trauma memories are situated mostly in the nonverbal right brain, and thus traditional talk therapies typically have limited success, at least initially. You'll also apply the principle of reconsolidation as you rewire your brain with many of the skills in this workbook.

Should You Consider Trauma Therapy?

As you undertake your healing journey, you might consider whether or not you wish to enlist the aid of a mental health professional, specifically a trauma therapist, to help you settle the aftereffects of ACEs. A skilled trauma therapist is like a coach or a guide. World-class athletes typically have a coach to provide perspective, to teach or reinforce needed skills, and to give moral support. A seasoned guide can help you get more out of a journey. Similarly, seeking a skilled mental health professional is like finding a coping coach or a guide to greater resilience. Seeking the right mental health professional is an act of wisdom that can speed recovery and alleviate needless suffering. You don't have to suffer needlessly for decades, because trauma specialists are discovering every year more and more effective ways to heal hidden wounds.

The natural tendency is to avoid painful memories. We do this by numbing emotions, denying that the past still hurts, or covering the pain through addictions (drugs, gambling, shopping, work, and so forth). However, avoidance leaves the memories untouched and likely to intrude into awareness in uncomfortable ways. The goal of therapy is to bring the memory forward, neutralize its distressing aspects, and put the memory fragments together. Then the traumatic memory can be stored like *one* memory alongside the other memories in the file cabinet, not the *only* memory sitting on the desktop.

You might feel comfortable trying the skills in this workbook on your own. Or, you might decide to find a therapist who can support you as you master these skills and deal with particularly distressing memories or symptoms. The remainder of this chapter will help you determine whether a trauma therapist might be right for you.

Does Therapy Work?

Yes, it does. Good therapy can lessen trauma symptoms and lift self-esteem. For example, trauma therapy for sexually abused children and adolescents has been found to improve self-esteem (Harvey and Taylor 2010). Therapy changes gene expression (Schore 2012), resulting in a calmer brain.

Quite often, trauma survivors "fear that they are damaged to the core and beyond redemption" (van der Kolk 2014, 2). Perhaps an unsuccessful experience with a psychotherapist in the past led you to believe that nothing can help. However, my experience tells me that there is no hole so deep or dark that one cannot climb out of it, especially with the right help. Again, love—along with calm and safety—is the healing agent. Mature love replaces fear and binds hidden wounds. As Lewis and colleagues stated (2000, 169), "Love is not only an end for therapy; it is also the means whereby every end is reached." And what is true for surgery is true for therapy: "Only human love keeps this from being the act of two madmen" (Richard Selzler, MD, quoted in Lewis, Amini, and Lannon 2000, 190).

When to Consider Therapy

You might seriously consider therapy if you are still suffering and struggling, and time has not provided sufficient relief. Symptoms might have even worsened over time. If you're unsure whether therapy might help, ask yourself if any of the following symptoms sound familiar, and know that therapy can help address them all.

- You can't think of certain memories without intense distress.

- You experience memory intrusions, including nightmares, flashbacks, or hallucinations.

- You or your surroundings seem unreal.

- You drift away mentally during stressful times.

- You experience disturbing emotions on a frequent or chronic basis. These can include crushing feelings of low self-worth, shame, guilt, fear, depression, irritability, or extreme anger. Being negative or harshly self-critical can reflect unresolved inner pain.

- You feel numb, unable to experience happy feelings.

- You have a mental illness, such as anxiety, panic disorder, depression, or bipolar disorder, that willpower alone is not helping.

- You are harming or are about to harm yourself (for example, cutting or otherwise injuring your body; having suicidal thoughts or behaviors; not taking care of yourself, such as avoiding needed medical care; having poor sleep, eating, or exercise habits; or having unprotected sex; engaging in risky behaviors such as driving dangerously or while intoxicated).

- You have an addiction—such as to drugs, alcohol, gambling, eating, or work—along with trauma symptoms. (Look for a therapist who can treat the addiction as you process the traumatic memories.)

- You can't function at home or on the job (for example, you have trouble concentrating or doing simple tasks; you avoid people or places you need to be).

- Stress is interfering with your sleep; you have excessive daytime fatigue.

- Relationships are being harmed by patterns formed earlier in life.

- You sense that something from the past might be damaging your mental or physical health.

- Any memories or symptoms seem overwhelming.

- Any topics or activities in this book are destabilizing.

Guidelines and Expectations

The process of healing is usually gradual. Most people experience substantial benefits within the first few months of treatment, although treatment lasting nine to twenty-four months or longer is often recommended, depending on such factors as the nature of the trauma, your support system, and your present level of resilience. (Some promising treatments may provide substantial benefits in much shorter periods.)

Individual therapy is usually the best starting point, although being part of a group can support the healing process. Most therapies start by educating about trauma and its impact. Skills are then taught regarding safety and stabilization, emotional and arousal regulation, self-esteem, relationships, processing memories, and transitioning to a fuller life.

Seeking help might be challenging if you have learned to distrust others, if you came to believe that no one wants to listen or help, or if you feel undeserving of happiness. So you'll want to shop for a therapist that you are comfortable with. Allow time for trust to develop, remembering that no one is perfect. Interview prospective therapists. Ask how they treat childhood trauma. They might describe childhood trauma as developmental trauma, interpersonal trauma, or complex relational trauma.

Proven and Promising Trauma-Processing Treatments

Relating your story in words and replacing unreasonably negative thoughts calm the arousal centers of the brain and help complete the healing process. However, trauma memories, which are situated in the visual, emotional, and survival brain regions, might initially be inaccessible to words and logic. Therefore, many of the effective treatment modalities do not rely primarily on words and logic. Rather, they access implicit memories with minimal or no verbalizing. Below is a sampling of some of the many effective treatment options. See the "Recommended Resources" section for more information on locating a therapist.

Body-Based Therapies

In this approach, the therapist helps bring the client back to optimal arousal levels, where stress levels are neither too high nor too low. In this window of tolerance, you are hardwired to talk calmly and logically, regulate emotions, and feel connected to your body. Storytelling takes a back seat to what is going on in your body. The therapist monitors subtle changes in your body and might say, "Let's put telling your story aside for a moment. It looks like your shoulders tense when you talk about that memory. Pay attention to that." Simply tracking what is going on in the body helps calm physical and emotional arousal and restores a sense of connection to the self. (Recall that under excessive stress, the brain kicks in to survival mode. In the urgency to fight or flee, areas of the brain concerned with logic, speech, and feeling connected to the self go off-line. Tracking helps bring these areas back online.)

The therapist might also say, "Think of a strength or other resource that helped you get through all that. Notice how your body feels as you think of it. How does that feel emotionally? Let that settle in your body." Or the therapist might suggest, "It seems like your body wants to complete an action that you weren't permitted to complete back then. I wonder what would happen if you planted your feet firmly on the ground and from the strength of your core slowly pushed back against the perpetrator." The client slowly completes the action impulse and tracks how that feels in the body. Now, action replaces the freezing state that was locked in the memory. Such body-based approaches have been pioneered by Bessel van der Kolk (2014), Patricia Ogden (Ogden and Fisher 2015; sensorimotor psychotherapy), and Peter Levine (2010; somatic experiencing).

Expressive Arts

Art therapy can be very effective. Often the hand expresses what the mouth can't. Once you put traumatic memory material at a safe distance—say, through drawing or sculpting—you'll likely find it easier to put words to the feelings. The Instinctual Trauma Response™ (see Intensive Trauma Therapy in the "Recommended Resources" section) is one excellent treatment method that combines art with video recording to gently and relatively quickly process traumatic memories in a way that is well tolerated.

Eye Movement Desensitization and Reprocessing

In eye movement desensitization and reprocessing (EMDR), the therapist asks you to recall a disturbing memory—and the associated emotions, bodily sensations, images, and thoughts. You then watch the therapist's fingers move back and forth in front of your eyes. Stimulating both sides of the brain through eye movements (or other forms of bilateral stimulation) is thought to help connect the memory to healing elements stored elsewhere in the brain. For example, the frightening image of a perpetrator might shift, or you might begin to experience more pleasant bodily sensations, emotions, or thoughts. Processing one memory might cause other memories in need of processing to come to awareness. The process continues until past memories are no longer disturbing. This can happen fairly quickly, depending on the nature of the traumatic memories.

Accelerated resolution therapy (ART) is a creative, effective therapy that also uses eye movements. ART can work quite quickly—sometimes within one to five sessions over a two-week period. In this treatment, traumatic memories are settled in a process similar to EMDR. In addition, the old image is replaced by a new preferred image that you create, along with new bodily sensations. Treatment is deemed successful when only the new image is recalled, although the original scene remains in the memory without the disturbing emotions.

Emotional Freedom Technique

Like EMDR, the emotional freedom technique (EFT) calls up the various aspects of the traumatic memory, followed by tapping acupuncture meridians. One theory is that tapping these points unblocks stuck energy and emotions. Stimulating both hemispheres of the brain is also thought to integrate the traumatic memory with healing thoughts and memories already stored in the brain.

Emotionally Focused Couple Therapy

This treatment modality helps couples strengthen attachment bonds between partners. It can be very useful when attachment insecurities from earlier in life are causing relationship problems.

Finding Treatment

The "Recommended Resources" section describes additional trauma treatments and will point you to ways to find a trauma specialist. Be willing to interview therapist candidates. Make sure they will let you control the pace of therapy, that they know how to help you process the memories you've experienced, and that they can teach the skills you'd like to learn, including those you are reading about in this workbook. Also, sense if you would feel comfortable working with them. Remember that if one therapist or one treatment modality isn't working for you after a fair trial, there are many, many other treatment modalities and therapists to try.

There is so much hope for healing your wounds from the past. The self-managed skills in this workbook, which are based on the foundation of rich clinical experience, will help you rewire your brain in positive ways—soothing old memories, calming your nervous system, and changing the way you experience yourself for the better. Start when you are ready, and take your time. Go at your own pace. If the going gets too difficult, ease up or find a trauma specialist to support your healing journey and skills practice.

Before moving on, do the following exercise to further contemplate your healing journey and the possibility of seeking competent professional help. A copy of this worksheet is also available at http://www.newharbinger.com/46646.

You might also wish to explore relatively new, professionally managed therapies that help to reboot and heal the brain that is damaged by toxic stress and inflammation. These promising therapies, which include transcranial magnetic stimulation, neurofeedback, gamma light flicker therapy, and various periodic fasting protocols, are usually used in combination with psychotherapy and self-managed strategies such as those in this workbook to reduce a wide range of psychiatric and medical symptoms (Nakazawa 2020).

In addition, please note: Although this workbook is written primarily for adults, it is helpful to know that children and adolescents also respond well to trauma therapy, even with high ACE scores. Some therapies involve nonoffending parents or caregivers, helping them to parent and manage their own distress and better support the child.

Considering Therapy

1. As you think about the considerations for therapy listed on pages 47–48, are there troubling symptoms you'd like to change?

_____

_____

_____

_____

2. How might your life be different if the troubling symptoms improved?

_____

_____

_____

_____

3. If you were to seek help, how would you describe the mental health professional that you'd most like to work with? What traits and skills would describe that person? What type of therapy?

_____

_____

_____

_____

Self-Care

CHAPTER 5

Regulate Stress Arousal

Taking care of yourself sends a strong signal to your brain that you matter, that you are worth the time to tend to your needs. People often ask me for effective, everyday coping tools that are quick and easy to master. Throughout the course of using this workbook, and throughout your life, you'll frequently need such tools to calm your nervous system, lift your mood, and be at your best.

In this chapter, I will introduce powerful tools to help you regulate your stress levels, because dysregulated stress is at the core of hidden wounds of ACEs. In the next two chapters, we'll explore skills to regulate strong emotions and ensure that your brain is in the best possible working order. Mastery of these skills is key to your success, because you will employ and build upon these skills in later portions of this workbook. Let's start with a very effective skill that you can practice at the start and end of your day to calm yourself and lift your mood.

The Five-Minute Foot-to-Head Stress Reducer

This skill is one of my favorite stress reduction exercises and is inspired by the excellent writings of Childre and Rozman (2005), Ogden and Fisher (2015), Satchidananda (2008), Shapiro (2012), and Steele (2007), among others. It is practiced first thing in the morning to start the day on a calm and pleasant note, and last thing at night to prepare for a restful, pleasant sleep. This strategy combines key elements of tried-and-true practices from around the world. For example, a single-minded focus calms the racing mind. Tracking the body—such as being deeply aware of breathing, heart rate, and bodily sensations—calms and synchronizes the various regions of the brain and the organs of the body. Activating positive emotions such as loving-kindness and cheer changes the functioning of the brain and body in beneficial ways. As with other scripts in the workbook, you can read and apply these instructions one at a time, have someone read them to you, or record and then listen to them.

Instructions

1. Sit or lie down on your back in a comfortable place.

2. Find an interesting spot on which to intently focus for a few moments. This could be a spot on the ceiling or wall or a spot of light. Then close your eyes, if that is comfortable (if not, you can simply lower your gaze).

3. Ground in your body. If you are sitting, feel the soles of your feet securely planted on the ground. Notice the sensation of the chair supporting your back and buttocks. If you are lying down, notice the sensation of your calves and buttocks against the surface.

4. Place your hands over your belly with your fingers spread out and separated. For a few breaths, sense the miracle of breathing—your belly expanding as you breathe in, and sinking as you exhale, like waves gently flowing in and out from the shore. Let your breath slow down naturally. Now imagine breathing loving-kindness—compassion or love—into your belly on the in-breath. On the out-breath, let loving-kindness settle in your belly.

5. Placing your hands over your heart, breathe compassion—loving-kindness or love—into your heart on the in-breath and let that feeling settle there as you breathe out.

6. Place your palms over your eyes and feel the warmth bathing and soothing your eyes. Gently rub your fingertips in a way that feels good against the hairline area, and then rub your thumbs gently over your temples. Lower your hands slowly, allowing your fingertips to rub gently over your forehead, eyes, and cheeks. Notice the sensations as you do so.

7. With the soft pads of your index and middle fingers of both hands, tap slowly and gently twenty-five times on the bone just beneath your pupils. Then rest your hands over your heart.

8. Think of a place, person, or time when you felt safe, comfortable, calm, or content. Recall what that felt like in your body. Let your face break into a warmhearted half-smile with a twinkle in your eye. Sense a pleasant, happy feeling surround your mouth. And that happy feeling spreads to your eyes—softly bathing and soothing your eyes. That pleasant feeling then slowly spreads to your forehead, temples, and top of your head—warming and soothing those areas in turn. That pleasant, happy feeling then moves down your neck and spreads through your shoulders, and down your arms and into your hands and fingers. Sense that. Now that happy feeling spreads down your spine like a warm light, and radiates outward—to both sides of your back, to your heart, lungs, belly, and pelvis—and then down your legs and feet. Sense that in your body.

9. Placing your awareness in your belly, release, rest, and relax in your true, happy nature for a few moments. Your true, happy nature is your core, your essential spiritual self that exists beneath your racing thoughts and feelings. It is kind, wise, and good-humored. You don't have to create your true, happy nature—it already exists within. You have only to take a few moments to experience it. Release, rest, and relax.

10. Place your right hand on your left shoulder. Place your left hand on your right shoulder. Gently squeeze the right shoulder as you say or think the word "safe." Gently squeeze the left shoulder, saying or thinking the word "calm." Repeat the alternating shoulder squeezes four more times, repeating the words "safe" and "calm." Then squeeze both shoulders slowly at the same time as you slowly repeat the word "secure."

11. Placing your hands over your heart again with your thumbs locked, think of someone who made you feel safe and loved. Let the feeling of love rest in your heart as you breathe. Slowly tap the region around your heart five times with the fingers of both hands as you silently say the word "love" with each tap.

12. Take a few moments to track your body and feelings. Let any pleasant feelings or sensations linger for just a few moments.

If time permits, you might take more than five minutes for this exercise. For example, if you notice that there is a part of your body, such as the forehead, that feels tense or uncomfortable, you might wish to allow more time to let the pleasant, happy feeling penetrate and bathe that part.

Now I'll introduce effective skills to manage stress arousal during the rest of the day.

Body-Based Skills

In our culture, we traditionally value logical thinking and speaking. However, experiencing or remembering toxic stress can take our thinking and verbal areas of the brain off-line. When this happens, logic and words are usually ineffective as tools to help us calm down. Thankfully, in recent years we have learned that there are effective ways to calm arousal—by targeting the body and the regions of the brain that control arousal—so that we can again think and speak rationally.

When stress arousal is in the resilient zone—neither too high nor too low—we are hardwired to think and speak clearly and rationally. Thus, we might figure out ways to solve problems, seek and offer support to self and others, or reason with difficult people. All parts of the brain and organs are working harmoniously. Breathing and heart rates are slow and rhythmic. We feel grounded and centered. Stress arousal fluctuates smoothly, reflecting balance in the branches of the nervous system.

However, toxic stress can bump us out of the resilient zone. We can become stuck in the hyperarousal zone, remaining on high alert as the brain anticipates ongoing danger. In this zone, we become overly aroused, and the abilities to think and speak reasonably fly out the window. Preoccupied with surviving, the survival brain overrides the thinking and speaking regions in favor of generating strong emotions and immediate action. Heart and breathing rates become rapid and erratic. Muscles become overly tense. Alarm centers become overactive. In this zone, we commonly experience strong distressing emotions (such as anger, anxiety, or panic), nightmares, flashbacks, sleep disturbance, and problems concentrating.

If we are stressed long enough—or if we are severely overwhelmed, especially if the movement of fight or flight is thwarted—we might become stuck in the hypo-arousal zone. Here we become too numb— exhausted, frozen, shut down, or collapsed—to think or speak calmly. We might also exhibit slumped posture, a downward gaze, glazed eyes, a flat or depressed expression, shame, hopelessness, helplessness, and detachment from ourselves or our surroundings.

Some people alternate between hyper- and hypo-arousal. Others show signs of both extremes simultaneously, usually when they are transitioning to the hypo-aroused state. In either extreme, words and logic are not typically effective. Advice to calm down, relax, or get a grip usually doesn't work. The first goal becomes returning the brain and body to the resilient zone.

So we'll sample some very effective body-based skills to first regulate the body's arousal in order to bring all areas of the brain back online. These skills all rely on *tracking*—deeply sensing what is happening in the body. The simple act of tracking calms the emotional and survival brain and brings key brain regions back online. These regions manage decision making, speech, and emotional and physical arousal, while restoring a sense of connection to your body, emotions, and self. When stress seems to be getting the best of you, you can try these skills, pioneered by body-based master clinicians Patricia Ogden (Ogden and Fischer 2015; Ogden, Minton, and Pain 2006), Bessel van der Kolk (2014), Peter Levine (2010), and Elaine Miller-Karas (2015). Better yet, master these skills now, preventively, so that you call them up when you are beginning to feel stressed, before you reach the breaking point. The skills below generally work equally well for people whose arousal is too high or too low. For example, moving can release the energy that needs to be expended so that arousal can return to normal. This is helpful if you are stuck on hyperarousal. Movement can also reverse the numb, frozen state if you are stuck on hypo-arousal. If you wish to learn about additional body-based skills, see the "Recommended Resources" section.

Knead

Place one hand around the opposite wrist. Track what it feels like to squeeze your wrist and then release the pressure. Continue to track as you slowly slide your hand up and down your forearm…squeeze, release; squeeze, release. Take your time. Notice sensations on the skin and deep within the arm. Experiment to see what feels best—mechanical or soothing squeezes, fast or slow, firm or soft, deep or shallow. Then notice the effect on your body from doing this exercise. Does your body feel a little calmer? Is your breathing slower? Are your muscles less tense?

Ground in Your Body

Place one hand on the middle of your back, so that your fingertips are near your spine. As you breathe, track what is happening under your hand. You might notice your rib cage expanding and contracting as you breathe. Track what happens to your body overall and your emotions as you do this. Place the other hand over your heart and sense what is happening near that hand. Experiment with different kinds of touch—firm, gentle, or soothing. You might move the hand on your back to your belly, throat, forehead, or any other place that feels good. Track the region under this hand. Then notice what is happening in your body and emotions generally. What is happening to your thoughts as you do this?

Resistance

The stress response is designed to get us moving. If we do not move, the tendency to move—called an action tendency—becomes stuck in memory, perhaps showing up as tense shoulder or abdominal muscles. The antidote is to move, releasing the energy of fight or flight. This can help with hyperarousal. Moving can also help when you are feeling numb, to counter the collapsed state.

When stressed, stand and place one foot firmly behind the other. Bend your knees. Sense the strength in your core, arms, and legs. Slowly push with your arms, utilizing the strength in your core and legs (or push against a wall). Track what that feels like in your body.

Change Posture

Childhood adversity might have taught you to look down, slump, or hunch your shoulders. Current stress might reactivate these tendencies. This skill loosens the grip of, and gives you control over, these tendencies.

When you feel stressed, notice what your posture tends to do. Do you drop your head, slouch, or tighten certain muscles? Exaggerate these tendencies, and track your body and emotions as you do. Now do the opposite! Stand or sit up straight, straightening your spine, lifting your head, and slightly expanding your chest. Look confidently ahead. Track how that feels. Notice whether this shifts your emotions slightly. Go back and forth between the two postural extremes several times to reinforce your sense of control.

Other Arousal Regulation Strategies

Want to know more about additional body-based strategies? I especially like two strategies to shake off the stored energy of toxic stress—or to get us moving when numb and shut down. You can find more information about these in the "Recommended Resources" section at the back of the workbook.

- *Berceli's Tension and Trauma Release Exercises* are a series of seven exercises to release energy in the psoas muscle, which connects the lower spine to the pelvis and femur. This muscle contracts in both trauma and everyday stress. Seven exercises, taking fifteen minutes total, release this tension.

- *Ping Shuai Gong swing hands exercise* uses gentle swinging motions to release stress, get your body moving, and lift your mood.

Track Your Progress

Any of these skills can be used whenever you feel distressed—either in everyday life or when reminded of the past. Practice leads to mastery so that you can readily call upon these skills when needed. Practice the Five-Minute Foot-to-Head Stress Reducer at the beginning and end of your day for at least three consecutive days to give it a fair trial. Describe your experience in your Skills Record (see appendix A). Then try one or more of the body-based skills for at least three consecutive days each, and record your experiences on your Skills Record. Your entries will provide valuable data as you later look back to recall what has worked for you.

CHAPTER 6

Regulate Strong Emotions

Strong, distressing emotions can keep stress arousal high. If they are constant, such emotions can also lead to exhaustion and maintain negative wiring in the brain. So let's look at some skills to manage disturbing emotions resulting from ACEs and current stressors. You'll find these skills useful for everyday stress. You'll also use them together with the skills you'll learn later on.

It's quite normal to wish to avoid unpleasant emotions. Avoidance, however, leaves emotions, and the memories driving these emotions, unchanged. And with avoidance, we don't learn how to confidently face emotions with equanimity. Fear of emotions actually keeps the brain on alert, setting us up for stress conditions (Farnsworth and Sewell 2011). It's good to know that you can learn new ways to handle unpleasant emotions comfortably and confidently.

Mindfulness and Self-Compassion Meditation

It is now well established that mindfulness meditation significantly reduces psychological and physical symptoms of a wide variety of stress-related conditions. Mindfulness practice teaches us to simply watch what is happening in ourselves, but in a special way. First, we watch with compassion—also called loving-kindness, gentle friendliness, or love. Compassion—responding to our suffering with kindness—is a powerful antidote to emotional disturbance, one that changes our physiology in a number of beneficial ways. For example, compassion regulates the heart and causes the brain to release oxytocin. Oxytocin is called the "calm and connect" hormone because it reduces cortisol levels and promotes bonding with other people. Mindfulness practice also teaches us to sit with emotions in a nonjudgmental, accepting way. That is, we simply notice what we are feeling without trying to change, evaluate, or fix anything at the moment. We simply watch, with calm curiosity. For many of us, this is a new experience. Instead of thinking, "Oh no, this is awful. I can't bear to feel this," we adopt the attitude, "This is just a feeling. Whatever it is, let me feel it. A feeling is not who I am at the core." In this way, we soften to emotions. The only thing that changes is the way we *respond* to unpleasant emotions.

As effective as mindfulness practice is, the practice of self-compassion (Neff 2011) adds a new dimension to meditative practice. Many people learn to internalize harsh criticism from caregivers or others. As adults, we continue the learned habit of harshly criticizing ourselves. We might think we motivate ourselves by continuous self-scolding and faultfinding. However, beating ourselves up with harsh self-talk degrades self-esteem and functioning. In fact, those lacking self-esteem are much more self-critical than those who possess self-esteem (Gilbert and Procter 2006). Kristin Neff (2011) has found that a kinder approach is a much more effective motivator, one that calms unpleasant emotions more effectively. Self-compassion offers a very simple and powerful antidote to self-criticism. When we encounter a difficult experience that stirs up unpleasant emotions, we practice responding with four statements: 1) one that acknowledges that suffering is occurring (this is similar to compassionate, mindful awareness); 2) one that acknowledges that everyone suffers at times (we are all in the same boat, wanting to be happy and not suffer); and 3) two that bring compassion and deep caring to the present moment through statements such as, "May I bring compassion to this moment."

The meditation that follows combines mindfulness and self-compassion elements in a very beneficial way. As with other scripts in the workbook, you can read and apply these instructions one at a time, have someone read them to you, or record and then listen to them.

Instructions

1. Sit comfortably where you won't be disturbed for about twenty minutes. Place your feet flat on the floor, with your hands resting comfortably in your lap. Your spine is comfortably straight, like a column of gold coins, and your muscles are relaxed. Your body is like a majestic mountain—serene, secure, and unchanging, whether in sunshine or enveloped by storm clouds. (This is the meditator's posture.) Close your eyes if that is comfortable (if not, simply let your gaze drift down-ward). Rest in your body and in your breath in this moment of peace. Let your belly be soft and relaxed.

2. Notice your breathing. Sense what is happening in your body as you breathe. Perhaps you notice your abdomen rising on the in-breath and falling on the out-breath. What is happening with your ribs and chest? Your heartbeat? Does your breathing slow as you pay attention to this moment? What sensations do you notice in your nose, throat, and lungs? Just watch with kind curiosity, without trying to change anything. And when thoughts arise, as they will—"I'm hungry," "What's on my to-do list?" and so on—just notice them with pleasant curiosity, and then escort your awareness back to your breathing. If a thousand thoughts arise, patiently, gently, pleasantly, repeatedly bring awareness back to your breathing each time.

3. Now recall a moderately upsetting situation in the recent past, perhaps something that happened at work or with a family member, and the unpleasant feelings of sadness, rejection, disappointment with yourself, unworthiness, anger, worry, or any other feelings that arise. Make a space for these feelings. Give deep attention to the feelings without judging them. They are just feelings. Think, "*Whatever* I am feeling is okay; let me feel it." Invite these feelings in, as you would invite a friend into your warm home.

4. Notice where in the body you sense the unpleasant feelings—your stomach, chest, or throat, for example. Experience the feelings completely, with full acceptance. Don't think, "I'll tighten up and let these feelings in for a minute." Don't push them away. Rather, sit with these emotions with a soft and open heart.

5. To that place in the body that holds the upset, breathe in loving-kindness. Let compassion infuse and surround the pain. Bring compassion to this moment as you would to a beloved child who is crying. You embrace the child until the crying stops, and then the child returns to playing. Likewise, embrace the pain; relax into it. It may seem unusual to offer yourself love, but trust the healing power of love. Trust your ability to provide loving-kindness as you would to a friend who is suffering.

6. Place a hand gently over the region holding the upset. With a soft and kind facial expression—perhaps like that of a loving parent—slowly and deliberately repeat these four statements, either silently or aloud (Neff 2011):

   This is a moment of suffering.

   Suffering is a part of life.

   May I be kind to myself in this moment.

   May I give myself the compassion I need.

7. As you continue to notice your breathing, feel soothing understanding and kindness filling your heart and body with each breath. Repeat the four statements in step 6 several more times.

8. When you are ready, take a more intentional in-breath, breathing into the area that has been holding the upset. On the out-breath, let awareness of that region of the body dissolve. The feeling of loving-kindness remains in your heart. You might wish to say these statements silently or aloud: "May I be happy; may I be at ease; may I be whole."

9. When you have finished, notice whether the present moment is somewhat less distressing than a few moments ago. Paradoxically, sometimes this happens when we don't try to make it happen.

Tapping

Trauma experts Bessel van der Kolk and Charles Figley have found tapping techniques like the emotional freedom technique (EFT) and thought field therapy to be quite helpful for decreasing emotional distress. Although they are not as well researched as some other strategies, there is considerable enthusiasm among clinicians and those who have tried them. Tapping is easy to learn. There appears to be no risks or side effects; it either works or it doesn't. Theoretically, the technique shares some elements with EMDR. It helps overcome avoidance, releases emotional energy, stimulates both sides of the brain, and installs a positive, soothing thought.

In this tapping technique, adapted from Bray (2017), Craig (2013), and Figley (1995), you'll tap with the tips of your index and middle fingers, except as noted—firmly, but not hard enough to cause any discomfort. The tapping points are:

- **Side of the hand** (the fleshy part where you would strike when doing a karate chop)

- **Top of the head** (use four fingers, either the tips or the flattened fingers, to tap the top of the head, toward the back)

- **Eyebrow** (the edge of either eyebrow near the nose)

- **Side of the eye** (on the bone on the outside corner of either eye)

- **Under the eye** (1 inch below the pupil on the bone)

- **Under the nose** (between the top lip and the nose)

- **Chin** (midway between the bottom lip and the bottom of the chin point, in the crease)

- **Under the arm** (on the side of the body, 4 inches below the crease in the arm)

- **Collarbone** (place a finger in the "V" notch at the base of the throat and above the breastbone; drop the fingers down 1 inch toward the navel, then slide your finger over 1 inch to either side. Alternatively, tap with the flat of a fist about where a man would tie a tie.)

- **Little finger** (along the line where the fingernail meets the skin on the ring side of the little finger)

- **Index finger** (along the line where the fingernail meets the skin on the thumb side of the index finger)

- **Gamut spot** (make a fist and place the index finger of the other hand between the knuckles of the little and ring fingers; slide the index finger 1 inch down the back of the hand, toward the wrist)

Instructions

1. Think about or remember a situation that led to moderately distressing emotions. Describe the problem. For example, "I'm feeling anxiety" (or some other unpleasant feeling, such as anger, sadness, or embarrassment). Calmly and honestly notice where in your body you are feeling this emotion most strongly. If thoughts or images arise, notice these, too.

2. As you think about the emotions and sensations, rate the amount of distress from 0 (none) to 10 (highest possible). This is known as the Subjective Units of Distress Scale (SUDS). Write down the distress rating.

3. Form a *setup* statement as follows: "Even though I have this _____ (name the unpleasant feeling), I deeply and completely accept myself." Put energy especially into the last part of the statement. If this is too much of a stretch, you might prefer to say something like:

    Even though I have this _____, I'm open to feeling calm and safe, and releasing this emotion.

    Even though I have this _____, I choose to relax and feel calm.

    Even though I have this _____, I choose to relax and let it go.

4. Recite the *setup statement* three times while tapping the karate chop point.

5. To keep the problem in focus, say a *reminder* phrase while tapping, as you focus on the problem. A reminder phrase might be, "This anxiety" (or name the relevant unpleasant emotion). Tap the following points, about six to ten times each, in order:

    - Top of the head
    - Eyebrow
    - Side of the eye
    - Under eye
    - Under nose
    - Chin
    - Under arm
    - Collarbone
    - Little finger
    - Collarbone
    - Index finger
    - Collarbone

6. The gamut procedure is designed to engage parts of the brain that might help change the way you respond to the experience. Tap the gamut spot continuously as you do the following in order:

    - Close your eyes.
    - Open your eyes.

- Look down and left.

- Look down and right.

- Whirl eyes in a circle.

- Whirl eyes in the opposite direction.

- Hum any tune.

- Count to five.

- Hum again.

7.   Repeat steps 4 and 5 again.

8.   Rerate the upset and write down the new SUDS rating. Track what has changed in your body or emotions.

9.   Repeat steps 4 through 8 until a SUDS rating of zero is reached, or there is no further drop in the upset. If there is a partial reduction in the rating, you might wish to modify the setup statement to one of the following:

Even though I have some remaining anxiety, I deeply and completely accept myself.

Even though I have some anxiety, I know what calm feels like.

Even though I have some anxiety, I choose to feel safe and let it go.

If you are in public and tapping is awkward, you might try this technique by just substituting a light touch on inconspicuous places. If this technique is not effective, either bypass it, seek help for processing the difficult event with a trauma specialist, or go to http://www.eft-alive.com/eft-article-when-eft-does-not-seem-to-work.html. The EFT website will direct you to break down the distressing event into specific aspects to process, and then you'll separately process the various emotions that arise.

The Pass-Through Technique

Singer (2007) has written that we each experience people, objects, events, emotions, sensations, and thoughts. But we are not any of these. Our inner spiritual self observes these from deep within. This strategy moves negative feelings that are bottled up from a few hours to many years ago, like moving stale air through the house. The energy of emotions passes through the heart. If the heart is not open, energy can be blocked, circling around and getting stuck. So this strategy teaches us to open the heart and let emotions flow through so we can again experience the beauty, joy, enthusiasm, and love that are behind the pain. When something reminds you of an unpleasant past event, smile, relax, watch it from a distance, and let the old stuff pass through you. Simply let it go without a struggle.

Instructions

1. As you prepare to recall an unpleasant event, focus on your breath. Close your eyes (or lower your gaze). Open and relax your shoulders and relax your heart. Perhaps you even smile as you anticipate the opportunity to release unpleasant feelings.

2. Don't be surprised if watching an unpleasant past event is uncomfortable. The memory of an unpleasant event is stored with pain. It is also released with pain. You must decide whether you want to continue to walk around with the pain or let it go. Letting it go will only hurt for a moment. It is usually not as bad as you think it will be.

3. Just be aware of the unpleasant memory. Watch old negative feelings come up without pushing them down or fighting them. Let them pass through your heart. For example, for embarrassment, you might allow the feeling to be and think: "What do people think of me? Let them think whatever they want. What does it matter? I'll watch the feelings and then let them flow out through my heart." Or, "Insecurity? It's just a feeling. Let it go." Each time you relax and release, a piece of the pain leaves forever.

4. Remember you are the one watching from the very center of your consciousness. The memory, with its emotions and sensations, is "out there," at a distance. Relax and release it. Let the pain come into your heart and pass through it. As long as you are watching from deep within, you are not getting lost in the distressing feelings. It's that simple.

5. You might end by repeating the four self-compassion statements on page 62.

Track Your Results

Try each of these emotional regulation skills in turn. Practice one skill daily over a three-day period before proceeding to the next one. Log your experience in your Skills Record (see appendix A). Which would you consider using on a regular basis? Remember, as you practice and master these skills, you'll be rewiring your nervous system to be less reactive. You'll also be adding to the skills that you can use to later heal the hidden wounds from ACEs.

CHAPTER 7

Take Care of Your Brain

Most of us do not fully realize how the physical condition of the brain profoundly affects our emotional well-being and our ability to heal from ACEs. If we did, we'd undoubtedly maintain our brains at least as conscientiously as we maintain our homes and cars. Researchers have discovered ten pathways to strengthen the brain, typically in a matter of weeks. Applying these steps will help you lift your mood, feel more rested, increase your energy, and prepare the brain to reap greater benefits from the strategies we'll explore later.

The ten pathways work together to improve the size, health, and functioning of brain regions that regulate emotions, improve thinking, and process memories so that they can be stored and retrieved in a cool, rational manner. In addition, these steps work together to:

- Promote the growth of new neurons and neural circuits

- Strengthen the blood–brain barrier, thereby protecting the brain against toxins

- Clear harmful substances from the brain

- Protect against damage to brain cells from oxidative stress and inflammation

- Protect telomeres and favorably influence epigenomes

When your brain is healthy and highly functional, you can more readily rewire it in beneficial ways. So you might think of this chapter as preparing your brain for the greatest possible success with the skills you'll later learn to heal from and move beyond ACEs.

The Big Three

Many people say they are surprised at how effective it is to make and stick to a nutrition, sleep, and exercise plan. Although they have often *heard* about how important these things are, actually implementing them makes a profound difference in how they feel and function. Perhaps you'll also find this to be true. Compare how you are doing with your nutrition, sleep, and exercise to the guidelines that follow. At the end of the chapter, you'll make a plan to optimize these factors and improve the condition of your brain.

Nutrition

Studies consistently support the conclusion that Mediterranean-style eating optimizes brain health and function. Visualize a plate full of plant foods—vegetables, fruits, beans, lentils, nuts, seeds, whole grains, and just about any herb and spice (except salt). Fish or other seafood occupies a smaller portion of the plate. Eggs and sometimes poultry can substitute for fish. Healthy fats, like olive oil, are consumed instead of animal fats. Dairy—including less than full-fat or fermented products such as yogurt, feta, mozzarella, and Manchego cheese—are eaten frequently in moderate amounts. Rarely eaten are red meat, processed foods (including hot dogs, ham, sausage, deli meats, refined grains, commercial baked goods, and desserts), sugar, salt, cream, margarine, and butter.

Plants provide fiber, vitamins, minerals, and antioxidants that are key to brain health and function. Americans generally fall far short of the 2½ to 3 cups of vegetables and 1½ to 2 cups of fruits per day that are recommended for most adults.

There is growing research interest in the microbiome, the community of 100 trillion bacteria living inside the human intestine. Certain harmful bacteria create inflammatory toxins and promote weight gain. On the other hand, helpful bacteria promote leanness and create 90 percent of the body's serotonin. Serotonin is a neurotransmitter that helps counter depression and anxiety, both of which correlate with self-esteem. The vagus nerve connects the gut to the brain, permitting two-way messaging between these organs. Eating fibrous plant foods, such as fresh or frozen fruits and vegetables and whole grains, promotes a healthy balance in the microbial ecosystem. Eating fermented foods, such as yogurt, kefir, sauerkraut, kimchi, and fermented cheeses, also helps. (In addition, exercise and managing stress help balance the microbiome.) Conversely, healthy balance is disrupted by consuming unhealthy fats, processed carbohydrates, and antibiotics.

And don't forget to stay well hydrated. Relatively small losses of bodily fluid can disrupt mood and mental functioning. Water, or in moderation low- or no-fat milk, is usually a good choice. Urine that is clear or pale yellow usually indicates sufficient liquid intake, while urine that is the color of apple juice or darker suggests the need for more liquid. Energy drinks are usually not a good choice. In the lab, a single serving of energy drinks can result in immediate improvements in cognitive and physical performance. However, when consumed regularly (two or more per day), energy drinks increase stress symptoms, including some that they purport to suppress: fatigue, sleep problems, depression, anxiety, aggression, and trauma symptoms. Even more moderate use—from one energy drink per week to one per day—is associated with symptoms of depression, fatigue, and aggression (Tobin et al. 2018).

Sleep

Most American adults are sleep deprived, falling well short of the seven to eight hours or more required for optimal mood and brain function. Sleep deprivation is a huge stressor, causing an increase in cortisol secretion. Excess cortisol secretion, in turn, causes symptoms of stress, depression, and anxiety. Sleep deprivation also results in the brain's emotional centers becoming 60 percent more active (Epstein 2010).

Thus, if you are feeling stressed, agitated, anxious, or down, take care of your sleep needs. Sometimes, getting as little as twenty to thirty minutes more per night yields large dividends.

In addition to getting a sufficient amount of sleep, strive for regularity, meaning go to bed and get up at the same times each day. This helps strengthen the sleep cycle in the brain, which tends to weaken with age.

Sleep quality is the third factor in good sleep. Light in the hours before going to bed, especially blue light from electronic devices, disrupts the natural sleep cycle and suppresses melatonin, while early morning exercise in the sun tends to solidify sleep. Try turning down the lights and turning off all electronic devices—television, smartphones, computer screens, and so forth—*at least* an hour or two before going to bed. Instead, wind down with soothing music, meditation, or calm reading. As a general rule, avoid eating within three or four hours of going to bed, as digestion can override sleep. Also avoid caffeine, nicotine, and alcohol, all of which disrupt sleep when taken in the hours before bedtime.

Exercise

It is well known that moderate exercise improves the mood and reduces stress, anxiety, and depression. Advances in neuroscience have uncovered numerous favorable changes in the brain resulting from exercise. If you are not presently exercising, you can work up very gradually to thirty minutes of brisk walking (or other continuous, rhythmic exercise like cycling or swimming) all or most days. To this aerobic base, you might wish to add strength and flexibility training for additional benefits. Find an exercise that you like to do. Make it enjoyable and not too strenuous and you'll be more likely to stick with it. Tai chi and yoga are other effective ways to stay fit and reduce stress. If you enjoy socializing, you might find a walking, tai chi, or yoga group.

The Other Seven Strategies

The big three—nutrition, sleep, and exercise—lay a solid foundation for optimal brain health and function. You can also expect significant gains from the following seven strategies.

Treat Medical Conditions

Certain common medical conditions can impair brain function and disrupt mood. For example, many people have a slight thyroxine imbalance, which can mimic depression and anxiety or worsen trauma symptoms. Thyroid-stimulating hormone (TSH) tests can determine whether thyroxine levels are right. If you are taking thyroid medication, frequent TSH tests can ensure that the dose is correct.

In sleep apnea, the airways collapse while sleeping. The brain might partially wake you up scores of times during the night in order to restore breathing. Often the awakenings are not remembered, but the oxygen-deprived person with sleep apnea feels fatigued, sleepy, and depressed during the day. Headaches, stroke, high blood pressure, and heart attacks are also linked to apnea. Apnea is common in people with PTSD. Treating the apnea often reduces symptoms, including nightmares.

Sometimes depression is linked to elevated cholesterol, which is often helped by lowering cholesterol levels through medicine or lifestyle changes. High blood pressure can cause microbleeds that damage the brain, so it is also important to control high blood pressure with medication or lifestyle changes.

Fortunately, all of these medical conditions are very treatable. Talk to your doctor to ensure that these conditions are ruled out or properly treated.

Minimize Pesticides, Pollutants, and Preservatives

Many chemicals in our environment are neurotoxic. Preservatives (found in processed foods) and pesticides (on produce) can be minimized by growing and preparing your own food or eating organic foods. Pesticides (and herbicides) might also come into the home on the bottoms of shoes that have been through treated lawns or golf courses. Pollutants in the home or car can be reduced by avoiding tobacco smoke, using good-quality air filters, and recirculating air within the car when in heavy traffic.

Maintain Oral Health

Treat and prevent gum disease to prevent toxins from entering the bloodstream and causing inflammation in the brain. Brush and floss daily, have professional cleanings, avoid tobacco, get sufficient sleep, and hydrate (stress dries out the mouth).

Minimize Anticholinergic Medications

Anticholinergic medications block a major neurotransmitter in the brain called acetylcholine. Examples of such medications include antihistamines, over-the-counter sleep aids, sleeping pills, tranquilizers, ulcer medications, and tricyclic antidepressants. Discuss with your doctor taking such medications no longer than needed, reducing the dosage, trying other medications, or trying nonpharmacological treatments (say, for depression or sleep problems; in the long run, nonpharmacological treatments for sleep problems work as well as or better than medications, without the side effects). Note that eggs are a good source of choline, which the body converts into acetylcholine.

Cut Out Drugs That Are Neurotoxic or Neuroinflammatory

Neurotoxic or neuroinflammatory substances include illegal drugs and the excess use of caffeine, nicotine, alcohol, and marijuana. Excesses of these drugs cause changes in brain function that are visible on brain scans years before anatomical changes occur. We might seek calmness and freedom from pain from a drug, but that gain is short-lived. When we find deeper peace, calm, and healing, such temporary fixes are no longer necessary.

Expose Yourself to Sunlight and Nature

Early morning sunlight helps regulate sleep and lift mood. This is why some people choose to exercise in the morning sunshine. During the cold and dark winter months, sitting in front of a light box that approximates the sun's spring morning intensity for up to an hour can help lift the mood of those who are sensitive to light deprivation.

Sitting or strolling in nature for twenty to thirty minutes three times weekly has been found to lower cortisol levels. Focus on noticing the sights and sounds, breathing fresh air, and becoming aware of other sensations. Avoid technology or even being distracted by focusing on aerobic exercise. Simply enjoy a nature break, letting your mind spin free, for a few minutes.

Manage Stress

When I see people in serious pain, my heart wishes for them a quick fix, one that provides permanent relief with no untoward side effects. I know of no pill that fits the bill. But I know of many healing strategies and skills, acquired over time, that can lessen suffering, lift our spirits, and often heal hidden wounds. The things that help are sometimes learned from a skilled therapist, sometimes through a healthy relationship, and sometimes through our own experiences and efforts. You've already learned some skills that can help you manage stress. In the chapters that follow, we'll explore what else you can do to manage stress, lift your mood, and heal damaged self-esteem.

Many people find that committing a plan to writing helps motivate and organize their efforts. As you review the ten pathways to take care of your brain, please make a plan that you feel you can stick with. You might use the form on the next two pages. Copies of these worksheets are also available at http://www.newharbinger.com/46646.

My Plan to Take Care of My Brain

The Big Three: Nutrition, Sleep, and Exercise

Nutrition

I'll follow a healthy eating plan by doing the following (making a written weekly menu on the following page will help you implement this plan):

_____

_____

_____

_____

_____

Sleep

I'll sleep _____ hours per night, going to bed at _____ and rising at _____, even on weekends. (Try to vary these times by no more than one hour from night to night.)

What I'll do to improve sleep quality:

_____

_____

_____

_____

Exercise

Each week, I'll do the following aerobic exercises (such as walking, swimming, or biking) or high-intensity interval training. Specify the days and amounts:

_____

_____

_____

_____

In addition, I'll do the following exercises for strength (such as resistance bands or weights) and flexibility (such as yoga or stretching). Specify the type, amount, and days:

_____

_____

_____

_____

_____

The Other Seven Strategies

I will do the following to take care of my health, minimize neurotoxins, get sunlight, enjoy nature, and manage stress:

_____

_____

_____

_____

_____

_____

_____

_____

My Weekly Eating Plan

On this sample menu, write down what food and drink you plan to consume each day and the amounts of each.

	Sun.	Mon.	Tues.	Wed.	Thurs.	Fri.	Sat.
Breakfast							
Snack							
Lunch							
Snack							
Dinner							
Snack							

Checking Your Eating Plan

After making your weekly eating plan, check how well your plan matches well-researched nutritional guidelines. Assuming you're an adult requiring about 2,000 calories each day, does your weekly plan provide:

- About 2 cups of fresh or frozen fruit and 3 cups of fresh or frozen vegetables in great variety?

- Adequate liquid? (You will likely need to drink at least 9 to 13 cups of liquid, depending on your size, activity level, and temperature. Water is an excellent choice for hydration.)

- About 5 to 6 ounces of healthy protein choices each day, such as fish, egg, poultry, dried beans or peas, nuts, or seeds? (Fish is especially good for the brain. Aim for at least 8 ounces per week. Most or all days should include nuts, seeds, and/or cooked dried beans and peas. Eat red or processed meats sparingly.)

- About 3 cups of low- or no-fat milk, yogurt, or calcium-fortified soy milk? (You can sometimes substitute 1 to 2 ounces of low- or no-fat cheese for 1 cup of dairy.)

- Mostly (or all) whole grains? (Whole grains contain more fiber, B vitamins, antioxidants, minerals, and beneficial plant chemicals than processed grains. About one-half cup of whole grains daily is a sensible goal.)

A nutritious eating plan will also minimize or avoid sugary, salty, processed, fatty, or fast foods, including soft drinks, sweetened fruit juices, candy, chips, pretzels, hamburgers on rolls made from white flour, baked desserts, whole-fat dairy, and butter. If you fill up on nutritious foods, it becomes rather easy to minimize or avoid these unhealthy foods.

Small Steps Make a Big Difference

This chapter has explained ten important pathways to optimizing brain health and function, in preparation for the skills you are about to learn. Try to do what you can, and don't be overwhelmed. Even taking small steps can result in noticeable gains rather quickly. For example, young adults with elevated levels of depression symptoms who followed a Mediterranean-style diet for three weeks showed significant reductions in depression, anxiety, and stress compared with those who did not change their diet (Francis et al. 2019). In another study, sedentary older adults with mild cognitive impairment who followed a diet similar to the Mediterranean diet and engaged in aerobic exercise only three times per week for six months experienced a nine-year reversal in brain aging (Blumenthal et al. 2019).

Strengthening and Stabilizing the Nervous System with Imagery

CHAPTER 8

Attachment Imagery

Happy childhood memories—fond recollections of affectionate parents—are associated with emotional well-being in older adults. On the other hand, toxic stress in the early years changes the circuitry in the developing brain. As we learned in the first section of this workbook, that process can start even *in utero*.

So the question is: What if you don't have fond memories of close relationships with your primary caregiver(s)?* Can negative neural patterns be rewired? The short answer is yes, because the brain is plastic, capable of changing and rewiring neural circuitry. However, this does not usually happen through insights or understanding alone. Memories of toxic stress play out not so much in the thinking and verbal regions of the brain, but in the visual, emotional, and visceral parts of the brain. As pioneering trauma researcher and psychiatrist Bessel van der Kolk (2019) notes, rewiring these memories requires strategies that are deeper than insights and understanding, which register in the left brain. What heals the traumatized brain is the felt sense of love, safety, and calm, which register in the right brain. Happily, evidence shows that imagery can make inroads to the areas of the brain that words and thinking do not touch. Because regulating the body helps regulate the brain, imagery can also impact the right brain indirectly by helping the body feel love, calm, and safety.

This and the next four chapters will explore imagery to strengthen and stabilize the nervous system, and to begin to rewire the brain. The main focus of these imagery exercises is to create new nurturing experiences rather than to directly modify old disturbing memories. In some cases, you will imagine being nurtured by ideal caregivers, thus mimicking healthy attachment experiences. In other cases, you will practice self-nurturing to create more positive neural circuits. So strengthened, you will be prepared in later chapters to directly rework unpleasant memories.

You might find that imagery is an unusual experience for you, perhaps one you have never tried before. So allow yourself some time to become accustomed to its practice. If the imagery that you practice does not square with your real-life experience, remember that in imagery, anything is possible. With focus and repetition, the neural circuits relating to the new image become stronger. Try to approach imagery with an open mind and heart. Cultivate curious interest, the attitude that trying to create a new experience *might*

---

* *Note:* As previously noted, the terms "mother" and "primary caregiver" are used interchangeably in this workbook. For the child, the preferred primary caregiver is usually the mother in the first eighteen months. However, caregivers might also be other helpers or family members. "Parent(s)" and "primary caregiver(s)" are also used interchangeably.

be beneficial. Then see what happens. You'll likely find that imagery becomes more and more effective and pleasant with practice.

Begin each of the following four imagery exercises by relaxing in a comfortable place, where you won't be disturbed as you practice. You might try any of the skills from chapters 6 and 7 to relax your body completely before you start. Practice the first imagery exercise for three consecutive days to give it a fair trial. As best as you can, concentrate and fully immerse yourself in the imagery. Most people find that closing their eyes helps maintain a soft focus. If closing your eyes is not comfortable, you can simply lower your gaze. Record your experience in your Skills Record (see appendix A). Then repeat this procedure for each of the next three imagery exercises. As with other scripts in the workbook, you can read and apply these instructions one at a time, have someone read them to you, or record and then listen to them.

In Utero Imagery

Recall that in the third trimester of pregnancy, infants can hear their mother's voice and experience physical sensations. It is logical to begin, then, with *in utero* imagery.

Instructions

Imagine, if you can, that you are an infant in your mother's womb. Your mother is resting from the preparations for your birth, rocking back and forth in her favorite rocking chair. You sense that she is content—happy with her life, feeling loved and supported by your father (or her partner). You hear her humming a soothing melody as she rocks back and forth. Your mother wants you and happily anticipates your arrival, and you feel that.

Your body feels comfortably nestled in her protective womb, cushioned, safe, and warm. You can hear your mother's rhythmic heartbeat and the other sounds of her body. Because she is at peace, you feel at peace. You feel at one with her—safe, secure, protected, cherished, wanted. And you sense what that feels like in your body.

Track what is happening in your body. What does your body feel like now? Notice your heartbeat, breathing, stomach, chest, and throat. What emotions are you feeling now?

Mother–Newborn Attachment Imagery

At the earliest age, children need to sense that they are affectionately bonded to their caregivers. Heart-to-heart communication is more important than words. Although children don't understand words in the first months of life, they sense and feel what is communicated nonverbally.

Instructions

Imagine that you are a baby in the first two years of life. You are in a pleasant place, perhaps your cheerfully decorated bedroom, or the cozy family room with a glowing fire in the fireplace. Imagine, if you can, a soothing, loving mother, who is kind, warm, and sensitive to your natural need to be loved and cared for. You sense that she is so glad to be with you. You hear her easy flow of speech and soothing sounds. Her voice sounds almost musical, like a soothing, cheerful melody. She is happy, confident, and at peace. At times you turn toward the playful quality of her voice. You trust her because she is good at heart. You know that she will take care of you. Her calm, secure presence calms you.

Imagine her lovingly cradling you. You feel the gentle warmth of her body and hear her soothing voice. Her body is relaxed, and this relaxes you. With fluid, even movements, she carefully and gently maneuvers you and adjusts you to keep you comfortable. You feel safe and close to her. You sense the rhythms of her heart and breathing...slow and easy. She softly strokes your forehead and rubs your tummy. You enjoy the feel of her skin as she touches your cheek with her soft cheek. She enjoys your baby smell and you enjoy the smell of her body.

And you turn to your mother's soothing and inviting voice, and see her face—smiling, joyful, bright, serene. And seeing the expression on her kind face...your eyes meet hers and you exchange loving gazes—feeling your hearts connecting and beating as one. You coo and smile in response to her playful gestures and sounds of her voice. And she smiles back. You sense inside that she enjoys being with you. You feel that you belong here. And your body relaxes...feeling safe...secure...loved. You are comfortable in silence. No words need be spoken. You rest safe and secure in her arms. You feel a sense of peace...of being loved...just as you are. And your heart "takes a picture" of this sweet, tender moment.

What's it like to know how happy your mother is to be with you? Does it feel safe, secure, content, peaceful, excited? Track this in your body. How does your body experience this? Notice all sensations and emotions.

Loving-Messages Imagery from Parents or Caregivers

Children need to sense that they are affectionately bonded to their caregivers. They need to receive messages, heart to heart, that signal they are loved and cared for. Even later in life, receiving these messages matters. It is interesting how life gives us opportunities to learn this.

Dana's Story

In an upper-level coping skills class, I was discussing the principle of loving messages, prior to practicing attachment imagery. Dana was a thirty-five-year-old returning student—bright, likable, and troubled by anxiety and low self-esteem. Thirty-five years earlier, her father had "deserted" her. Her mother had told her: "Your father abandoned you because you were a premature baby. He called you ugly and said he didn't love you. He's sick and all your faults are from him." Dana didn't return his cards and letters, fearing she'd betray her mother.

That weekend, Dana's father called. He was in the hospital dying of cancer several states away. He asked if they could talk. Dana reluctantly went, screwing up her courage and hoping the visit would be quick and painless. As she was driving, she thought, "What if he tells me I'm not good enough? What if he's a sick bum?"

When she arrived at the hospital, she found a loving, compassionate man. He explained that he had fought for custody of her and lost. He had become depressed but recovered and remarried well. He told Dana, "I thought you were the most beautiful, precious baby. I loved you and was so glad you were born. I wanted to take care of you, but the courts wouldn't let me." Dana and her father hugged and spent eight hours together.

When Dana returned to class that week, she was radiant. She had learned that her father wasn't a bad person. Neither was she. His messages were profoundly healing.

Dana was privileged to receive the loving messages that every person needs to hear in order to develop properly. Ideally, these messages are conveyed in the earliest weeks of life. However, imagery can help replace early memories that lack these loving messages. With repetition, the new memory circuits become more ingrained.

Instructions

This imagery weaves into memory messages that each person needs to hear. Imagine that you are in your third year of life and the verbal areas of the brain are developing. At this stage, the messages that you need to hear may be only partially understood in a literal sense. But their feeling tone can be imprinted until such time as their literal meaning is fully grasped. At this age, you are becoming aware of other important caregivers.

Imagine that you are resting comfortably in your cradle, perhaps in your cozy bedroom or family room by the fireplace. Imagine, if you can, two ideal parents beside you. Their gestures, postures, facial expressions, and voice tones let you sense that they enjoy each other's company, and that makes you feel calm and safe.

Imagine them gazing at you with eyes of love. Notice their loving facial expressions, soothing tone of voice, and comfortable body movements. They are fully present with you...completely focused and attentive. In their presence, you feel loved and wanted. Your eyes meet, and you return their loving gaze. Perhaps one gently rests a hand on your shoulder, while another rubs your hair or caresses your cheek. They smile, just enjoying your presence. And you smile...and feel close to them. Sense that in your body.

Imagine that they lovingly tell you these messages, alternating so that you hear them speak one after another. You hear the rhythm and pleasant tone in their voices as they speak these words:

Welcome to our home.

We are so glad you are here...so glad you are in our lives.

We wanted you to be born and to come to our family.

We're glad you are a girl (or boy).

You are precious and worthwhile to us.

We love you…right now…just as you are…the whole stinky, squirmy, wonderful package you are.

We will always love you…always!

The way we look at you, listen to you, touch you, and speak to you lets you know we love you.

You are so beautiful to us.

All our children are beautiful deep inside…and fun to be with. We enjoy being with you and spending time with you.

We love watching you grow up and develop.

We know you will be good and happy.

All your feelings are all right with us. Whatever you feel, we'll also feel. When you are happy, we'll feel happy with you. When you are crying or afraid, we will pick you up and hold you and comfort you…and you'll know that things will be all right. When you are angry, we'll soothe your pain.

We'll take care of you…love and protect you…and help you learn to take care of yourself.

You'll always carry our love in your heart and find comfort there.

They embrace you…a loving, soft, warm hug. And you feel a sense of ease. You smile as you ponder and enjoy this moment, and feel good and warm all over your body.

Check in with your body. Track your heart, breathing, gut, and other bodily sensations. Notice what is happening with your emotions.

New Baby's Arrival Imagery

If you felt neglected because your primary caregiver was preoccupied with another sibling, this imagery, inspired by McKenzie and Wright (1996, 117) can be useful.

Instructions

Imagine that a new sibling has just come home from the hospital. Your mother rushes to you and hugs you with delight. She is excited to see you, and you feel her delight. She tells you how much she's missed you. Then she asks, "Would you like to meet your new baby brother (or sister)?" Perhaps you peek at your new sibling with loving curiosity…and you smile. And you hear your mother say to you, "We'll always cherish you. If we welcome more children, we'll always love you the same. We adore you." You feel safe, secure, and loved. You sense that your parents are happy, secure, pleasant, and delighting in their interactions with you.

Track what is happening now in your body. What do you sense inside? What emotions do you feel?

Track Your Results

After practicing each of these imagery exercises once a day for three consecutive days and recording them in your Skills Record, review your Skills Record (see appendix A). Consider if you would like to repeat these exercises in the future to further imprint the wiring of these new experiences.

CHAPTER 9

Self-Nurturing Imagery

Self-nurturing imagery instills the pattern of being kind and supportive to yourself. If others have been unkind, you can choose to be loving to yourself. If you did not receive sufficient love from your caregiver(s), it is especially important to learn to become a good parent to yourself, to provide the love that was in short supply early on. This is a powerful skill to develop, one that changes the circuitry in the brain in positive ways. This skill complements trauma treatments. Whereas trauma treatment aims to neutralize troubling memories, the goal of this imagery is to soothe the nervous system by providing the needed nurturing that was lacking at the time (Steele 2007).

The next two imagery exercises focus on nurturing the imagined infant and changing the way you experience yourself. The imagined infant represents who you were at the core—and still are. Adjust the pronouns as needed to reflect the appropriate gender. As with other scripts in the workbook, you can read and apply these instructions one at a time, have someone read them to you, or record and then listen to them.

Self-Nurturing Newborn Baby Imagery

In this imagery, you will imagine visiting yourself on the first day of your life, in a safe place—the hospital's birthing room or nursery, a pleasant room at home, or any other safe place you'd like to imagine—providing all the nurturing for yourself that was needed then.

Instructions

Find a quiet place where you will be undisturbed for twenty minutes. Sit in a comfortable position. Take time to gather any negative thoughts that don't serve you and imagine them floating away, like smoke in the wind. Gently close your eyes and relax. Breathe easily and slowly. Release tension. Relax all areas of your body. Breathe again.

In a little while, you will be meeting the newborn that you were on your first day of life…because anything is possible in imagery. And you begin to prepare inwardly for that tender, precious encounter. With some satisfaction, you realize you have survived and overcome so much.

PERSPECTIVE OF THE GROWN-UP

Now you've come to nurture and support that little child. You are a grown-up now—strong, wise, and kind. And your deep intention is to take care of this little one. You know that whatever unwise choices you have made in the past really don't matter now, because that little baby only wants a grown-up who will love, protect, and keep her safe…someone who will delight in her presence…someone who is imperfect but sincere. You are that grown-up…you are good enough. Your quiet, loving presence is enough.

You know that that little infant will sense that you are safe and calm. So you take a moment to let your heart relax, to be warm and open…beating with calm regularity. As you think of the baby's simple needs, you know that you are very capable of meeting them. You feel confident.

And now you approach that infant. And there she is…lying in the cradle…how precious, how inno-cent…how full of awe and wonder! You slowly move toward that child with very natural, rhythmic move-ments, and calmly and gently reach to pick her up.

PERSPECTIVE OF THE BABY

Now imagine that you are that newborn baby. You are lying in the cradle, trying to adjust to all the newness of the world as well as you can. You sense that the adult who is greeting you is good, safe, and calm. And you find the adult's relaxed confidence and ease of movement reassuring. You are looking for goodness and love, and that is just what this grown-up brings you.

You are gently fussing, feeling a little uncomfortable. And you feel those strong arms gently pick you up and cradle you warmly, and you hear the soft, comforting tones of the grown-up's voice saying, "I'm here. I'm with you. I love you." As you gently rock back and forth, your body relaxes…you feel loved, safe, protected, and enjoyed. You sense that this grown-up is kind, good, capable…one whom you can trust. It feels delightful to experience these feelings, and to sense the grown-up's delight in being with you. You hear the grown-up's heartbeat, slow and regular, and you feel those strong arms gently cradling you, and that feels so comforting and peaceful. And the grown-up gently kisses your cheek and holds your little fingers… and you feel loved…content in this moment…and in your heart you feel tender love and trust for this grown-up. You feel secure…that you belong here in this world.

PERSPECTIVE OF THE GROWN-UP AGAIN

How lovely to feel that precious little baby nestled in your loving arms. And you feel at one with that precious infant, because you really are one. And you know that whatever happens in the future, you and that infant will go through everything together. You will always be there, fully present, always willing to work through difficulties together, with kindness…always taking delight in life's pleasures, great and small…always ready to keep your growing self safe and protected.

And for the next few moments, you simply enjoy feeling the warmth and closeness of that child, listen-ing to her breathe, and smelling her sweet baby smell.

And you know that wherever that child goes in life, you will be there…with love…encouragement…kindness…protection…and that that baby's life will be bright and good, with many moments of delight. And you feel whole. Your heart feels full of light and love.

Just sit there for a few more moments, with a sense of wonder and oneness with that precious newborn. Imagine both you and the child taking soft, relaxing breaths, breathing in love, hope, and peace. Breathing out, letting go of tension, worries, whatever doesn't serve you. Really, the two of you are breathing as one, and your hearts are beating in sync.

When you are ready, begin to move your body, moving your hands and fingers, arms, feet, legs…gradually moving more and more. When you are ready, slowly open your eyes and smile.

Track your responses to the exercise. What does your body feel like? Your emotions?

Bringing the Distressed Child Securely Forward

This imagery exercise implants the idea that no distressing situation need be permanent. There is light at the end of the tunnel. You can feel safe and keep your dream of a better life alive.

Instructions

Sit in a quiet place, where you can be undisturbed for about fifteen minutes. Relax your body as you rest in your breathing and release tension. Close your eyes if that is comfortable. Imagine that now you are in your first two months of life. Though you are still a baby, you are aware of the distress in your surroundings. And you wish for a sense of order…peace…harmony.

And see who is coming! It is that same reliable grown-up who greeted you earlier, in the previous imagery exercise. You recognize him…strong, wise, kind. It is your older self…who has grown into a capable, caring, trustworthy adult. He is so glad to see you, and you are glad to see him. And that grown-up gently reaches down for you and picks you up…warmly cradling you in those strong and caring arms, knowing just what you need. You feel protected, and your body begins to relax. He says in a very soothing way, "Come with me, child, as I bring you to a safer place and time." And together you go…forward to the present…gladly and trustingly…arriving at a cozy, pleasant room…feeling the pleasant warmth of a fire in the fireplace…and you hear soothing music playing in the background as you are held and rocked back and forth, back and forth, in those comforting arms.

The grown-up says with calm assurance in his voice, "You are safe now. You will never again be alone. There will always be at least one person who will be here to care for you—me. You can always count on me. I'll always love you, no matter what." Although you are too young to understand those words, you sense the sincerity of his caring. And that causes you to feel secure…peaceful…calm…hopeful. Just imagine how being warmly held in this safe place feels in the baby's body. Sense the emotions that your infant self is feeling and notice where in the baby's body those emotions are experienced.

And now imagine how good it feels for the adult you are to be holding that precious baby, feeling the weight of his warm, cuddly body, and to know that wherever that precious being goes, you will always care for him, always protect him, always seek the best for him. You feel a sense of wholeness. Let your heart and breathing be slow and regular as you enjoy these feelings for a few moments. And when you are ready, open your eyes.

Track Your Results

Try each of the two self-nurturing exercises for three consecutive days, recording your experiences in your Skills Record (see appendix A). In your journal, write about your experiences.

In the days ahead, consider what nurturing that infant needed, and imagine filling that need now as a caring adult, whether it is being held, giving reassurance, or providing love and encouragement.

CHAPTER 10

Exploring Imagery

Securely attached children experience their caregivers as a secure base, which provides the children with the confidence they need to venture out into the world, discover its delights, and find their way in this new, exciting realm. Reliable caregivers are also a safe haven to which the children can return when they need to refill their emotional well.

A learning process unfolds whereby children begin to balance the need for connection with the need for independence. When toddlers begin to explore and then become anxious, they will look back to their secure base—their trusted caregiver—for comfort and reassurance. As needed, they will return to their secure base, using their caregiver as a safe haven until they are ready to again branch out to explore the world. Stable relationships and supportive engagement with both mothers and fathers contribute in unique ways to confident exploration and adult adjustment, resilience, competence, and achievement (see Grossman et al. 2008).

The exploring imagery in this chapter builds upon and solidifies attachment imagery. The imagery exercises help replace anxiety, depression, self-dislike, and other symptoms of ACEs with a new sense of curiosity, confidence, and adventure. You'll imagine not a memory, but new scenes—creating new experiences of having a secure base and being open to enjoyment. You'll practice two types of exploring imagery: first, one with ideal, supportive parents and a second with self-nurturing. The latter approach reinforces the pattern of self-compassion. It can be especially useful for people who have difficulty imagining ideal parents. As with other scripts in the workbook, you can read and apply these instructions one at a time, have someone read them to you, or record and then listen to them.

Exploring with Ideal Supportive Parents as a Safe Haven

In this imagery exercise, you will practice what it might have felt like to have had kind, supportive caregivers who shared your joy in exploring and learning to confidently venture out in the world.

Instructions

Sit comfortably in a place where you will be undisturbed for about fifteen minutes. Rest, release, and relax in your breath. Let the gentle rhythm of your breath deeply relax your body as you let go of tension and any negative thoughts.

Imagine you are a toddler, perhaps between one and two years of age. Create a scene where you may playfully explore—a child's room with lots of toys, the garden, a park, the beach, or on a walk. This is your imagery, so you can pick whatever you wish.

Imagine one or both ideal parents—kind, loving, and fully present—sitting and watching you getting ready to explore. You sense that they are at peace…glad to be there, happy to be near you, and so pleased to be involved in your life…and that makes you feel safe, calm, and joyful. Visualize the scene in detail. Notice where you and they are. Notice your surroundings. What do you see, hear, smell, and feel against your skin? For example, if you are outside, what does the sunshine or breeze feel like on your skin?

The world before you is so interesting! You are curious to discover it. As you begin to move away to explore, you sense that they trust you and are so delighted that you are ready to explore your world. They allow you just the right amount of freedom to explore. Yet they are there, available for whatever you need—reassurance…comfort…encouragement…and safekeeping. You can tell they love you and enjoy watching you strike out on your own.

You look back at them and see their kind faces. The expressions on their faces let you know that they see you as capable…full of potential…able to find your way in the world…worthwhile. They smile and encourage you in a way that is just right for you. You hear them say, "Look at you go! That's wonderful that you are exploring. What fun!"

And you love exploring. You feel safe, protected, secure…knowing they are near. You feel confident and capable as you explore…curious, eager, full of life and enthusiasm. Notice what it feels like in your body to feel secure, loved, protected, and adventurous all at the same time.

After a while, you return to their warm embrace…just because it feels good. And you sense how that feels in your body to rest and be lovingly held in their arms.

And after a while, you go back to the joy of exploring, knowing that they are your safe haven. They have your back. They are looking out for you. You can return to them whenever you are afraid…whenever you need to be soothed…whenever you need to feel their love. They will be waiting with open, comforting arms. Sense in your body what it is like to be having fun exploring, knowing that they are watching out for you. What emotions are you feeling?

Exploring with Self-Nurturing

This exploring imagery is practice in providing self-nurturing to the naturally curious child. If needed, change the pronouns to the appropriate gender.

Instructions

Sit comfortably in a quiet place where you will be undisturbed for about twenty minutes. Take a few moments to relax your body. Notice your breathing…the rising of your abdomen as you breathe in and the falling of your abdomen as you breathe out. See how focusing on your breathing helps you clear your mind and helps your body let go of tension. In this relaxed state, prepare for a unique imagery experience.

FROM THE ADULT'S VANTAGE POINT

Imagine that the adult you now are is living in a very pleasant house. The backyard is very beautiful… the soft green grass is like a carpet. Around the yard are lovely trees. On this near-perfect spring day, you are sitting in a comfortable chair in the backyard. A gentle breeze and warm sunshine feel so good on your skin. The air is fragrant with blooming flowers. In this peaceful moment, you are holding the little toddler you once were—perhaps about sixteen months of age…because everything is possible with imagery. How precious that child is! How you enjoy feeling that toddler in your arms as he snuggles against your body and you feel his warm weight against you. For the moment, the toddler is quite content to be nestled against your body, enjoying the closeness. You love these tender moments, and you relish the thought that this young child is growing up so nicely…his little arms and legs are becoming strong and full of energy. After a while, the child begins to look around and fidget, and you know he would like to get down now, so you help him down.

TAKING THE CHILD'S PERSPECTIVE

Having soaked in the grown-up's love and comfort, you, the toddler, are so curious and eager to explore. You see a sandbox a short distance away and begin to move toward it. The cool green grass feels good under your toes. After a few steps, you pause and look back at your trusted grown-up. He is quietly smiling at you as if to say, "You're doing fine. How wonderful that you are exploring! Look at you go. Your little legs are so strong. Everything is all right. I'm right here when you need me. Enjoy your adventure." Satisfied, you continue over to the sandbox, eagerly get in, and sit down. You run your fingers through the sand. How interesting it feels! You put a little sand in the pail and lift the pail, feeling the strength in your little arms and being thrilled to discover what your body can do. You glance to see if the grown-up is watching. He smiles with a twinkle in his eye, sharing in your pleasure. And you go back to playing in the sandbox.

After being absorbed in your new discoveries for a while, you want to return to the grown-up, so you begin to walk back. And there is that trusted grown-up with a warm smile and welcoming expression. As you get close, the grown-up opens his loving arms to receive you. You smile at each other as he lifts you into his lap and snuggles you. Without words, you know that the grown-up likes being with you, and will be there to comfort, protect, and encourage you. It feels like you've come home. For the next few moments, you bask in the closeness you feel to that grown-up, who says, "I'm here, now and always, whenever you need me. I'll enjoy each step you take…there is so much that you will see and learn and do…so many good times ahead. We're going to enjoy this adventure called life together." You gaze into each other's eyes and smile at each other, so glad for this moment of being together again. The grown-up's presence and touch put you at ease. Just those few moments of closeness have given you just what you need…the security to venture out again.

After a while, you look around. Over there…you see the beautiful flowers in the flower bed! And off you happily go again to explore…knowing you'll return safely again to that trusted grown-up for comfort and security.

AGAIN FROM THE ADULT'S VANTAGE POINT

For just a few moments, enjoy the feeling of having nurtured your younger self's exploration. How wonderful that you have provided the security that is so important to a growing little person. You know that you and the younger self are really one and the same. You also know that you can be a dependable source of comfort and encouragement to yourself in any circumstance…good…bad…and in between. You know that you can supply love whether you are at your best or at your worst. Having been through difficult times, you've learned just what is needed…and you know how to comfort and nurture yourself.

Track what your body and emotions feel like and sit with those sensations and feelings for a few moments.

Track Your Results

Try each of these exploring imagery exercises for three consecutive days to see how they work for you. Record your experiences in your Skills Record (see appendix A). In your journal, you might explore: Is imagery becoming a more comfortable skill to practice? Are you allowing yourself the opportunity to create happier childhood experiences through imagery? Which type of imagery feels good to you—imagining ideal parents, self-nurturing imagery, or both? Can you imagine the possibility of noticing in the present moment what you need emotionally, and then meeting that need with calming, compassion, or soothing? Are there ways to change the imagery exercises to make them more effective for you?

CHAPTER 11

Attachment Imagery for Your Teen Years

As young people mature, they naturally become more self-reliant. Part of normal development involves separating from caregivers and becoming more independent. Secure attachment facilitates this transition, and healthy attachment needs do not go away. The healthy love of concerned parents continues to be important into the teen years and beyond. Yet for many adults, wounds from attachment disruptions in the teen years related to ACEs continue to sting. The imagery in this chapter will help create a new nurturing experience by providing the healing messages you needed to hear as a teen from your parent(s).

As with other scripts in the workbook, you can read and apply these instructions one at a time, have someone read them to you, or record and then listen to them.

Messages from a Loving Caregiver

In this imagery, you'll receive messages that each teen needs to hear. A teen's capacity to internalize verbal messages is more fully developed than a young child's, but the impact of these messages on the body is still important. Adjust the pronouns and references to the caregiver(s) in any way that feels right to you. For example, you might imagine spending time with one or two trusted caregivers.

Instructions

Find a comfortable place to relax undisturbed for about twenty minutes. Sit comfortably erect, like a dignified mountain that is unchanged despite the surrounding circumstances. Settle your mind by resting in your breath, just noticing the in-breath and the rising movement of the belly, and the out-breath and the falling of the belly.

Imagine ideal parents or caregivers, as you conceive them to be. Imagine that you and these parents are taking a long, relaxed walk on a beautiful day (or perhaps that you are taking a relaxing drive or sitting by the fireplace with them). You feel safe because they have always been ones you could count on...always there for you. Notice what your body feels like in this pleasant setting.

See what these parents look like as you walk. Notice what they are wearing…their postures…gestures…gaits…facial expressions. They have put all their concerns and tasks aside and now give you their full attention…and you feel secure in their company. Notice how it feels emotionally and in your body to be with these trusted, loving parents.

Imagine that these parents are comfortably near you, perhaps gently touching your shoulder occasionally, or placing an arm warmly around you, as you hear them alternately say the following. Pause to let each sink in, as you experience each statement in your body:

We love you just as you are.

We enjoy being with you.

We've liked raising you.

You are important to us.

We appreciate what you bring to our family.

We will always be interested in your life.

Your happiness is our heartfelt desire.

Be secure in our love. You don't need to prove your worth to us.

We respect your thoughts and your abilities.

We are cheering for you as you're finding your way in life.

We enjoy watching you discover your capabilities and interests.

At your own pace and in your own way, you're becoming a wise and caring person…able to uplift yourself and others.

When you stumble, we still love you and trust that you will right yourself.

We so appreciate how you respectfully treat yourself and others.

We're so glad that you live true to your conscience, even when that is difficult or unpopular.

We see you becoming an adult who belongs in the company of other good adults—as an equal, with your own opinions, expertise, and influence for good.

It's okay to separate from us.

We're delighted that you are becoming independent and finding ways to connect with others who treat you well and support you.

Your desires for attachment and wholesome intimacy are normal and natural.

We're glad that you're finding respectful, caring ways to grow love and intimacy.

We're glad that you're figuring out what matters most to you in life, what convictions and purposes are most fulfilling.

Remember, we will always love you.

You can visit or talk with us whenever you want. We'll try our best to help you make sense of difficult times if you ask us to.

Things in your life will turn out all right.

Track Your Results

Perhaps you smile to hear these messages. Notice what you feel in your body as you ponder them. Can you feel your heart soften? Your body relaxing? Pay attention to your breathing, your heartbeat, and your gut. What do you notice? What feelings does this imagery call up? As usual, practice this exercise once daily over a three-day period and record your experience in your Skills Record (see appendix A).

CHAPTER 12

Comforting Imagery for Difficult Times

We each go through difficult times in our mortal journey. No one is exempt. We are not equipped, nor are we expected, to go through such times alone. We all rely on others at times to help us meet our needs—to help us cope, to provide food, love, learning, protection, and encouragement. Young children, however, often encounter overwhelming ACEs when they are especially vulnerable—fending for themselves when brain areas and coping skills are not yet mature.

What if you could initiate the pattern of bringing comfort and kindness to your difficult times? The imagery in this chapter is a form of self-nurturing for a difficult time. As with other scripts in the workbook, you can read and apply these instructions one at a time, have someone read them to you, or record and then listen to them.

Comfort for the Hurting Younger Self

In this imagery, you will travel back to a time that you, as a child, suffered greatly. Only this time, the child receives what was needed back then to get through that difficult time in a constructive way. In this way, you create new programming—weaving in positive themes to reshape the programming from early toxic stress. At the same time, you build upon your ability to provide self-nurturing and support for difficult times in the present.

Instructions

Sit comfortably. Take a few easy, deep breaths and let go of stress. Close your eyes if that is comfortable. Now think back to a difficult moment in your childhood when you were really upset. Perhaps you were mistreated or neglected, or there was confusion around you, and you were feeling afraid, angry, embarrassed, lonely, or sad. When you have a time clearly in mind—either a specific event or a particular time period—then you are ready for this imagery. Keep this in mind as you go back in time to soothe it with love.

Imagine that you—as a kind, wise, strong, and more experienced adult—step into a time machine and go back in time to visit the hurting child: the younger you. When you step out of the time machine, you see each other. The child has been waiting eagerly for you and is so glad to see you! Your eyes meet. You feel a real affinity for each other, like two best friends seeing each other after a very long absence.

Take a long look at the child. How old is she? What is she wearing? Notice her facial expression and posture.

You see what is happening at this child's difficult time. You ask the child what she is experiencing and how she feels. You listen with great love, empathy, and respect. "No wonder you are upset," you say. "This is a difficult thing for a child to experience alone. I'm glad you've coped as well as you have."

You ask the child what she needs. Again, you listen with great love, empathy, and respect. Perhaps she needs an embrace, a touch, or an arm around the shoulder and the wordless assurance that everything will be all right. And you provide that. Maybe she needs to hear encouraging words like, "You're going to get through this." If she needs physical protection, you stand in front of her and provide it. Perhaps you help her say what she didn't know how to say back then, such as "Stop! I am worthwhile, and that's no way to treat a child." Perhaps you recognize a need that the child can't express with words and you take charge and meet that need. Perhaps she just needs to know that you are there beside her and that she is not alone…that she is loved…for we can get through anything if we know that.

The younger self feels comforted and safe in the love that you communicate through your eyes, your expression, your gestures, and your heart…by the way you look at her, speak to her, touch her, and protect her.

Before leaving, you let her know that you won't leave her alone, that you'll be here to provide the love and help she needs—*whenever* these are needed…in good times or bad, when she is at her best or worst. Perhaps no words are needed to communicate this. Perhaps you explain: "This difficult time does not define you…there is so much more to you than what you went through…see how you are surviving that difficult time back then…I'll help you find your way through every difficult time…I'll remind you to let go of negativity so you can enjoy the many pleasant moments ahead." Perhaps you say, "I know you'll go forward with inner peace and confidence, knowing that you're worthwhile, loved, and capable of living a good and happy life."

It's time to return to the present now. Perhaps you bid farewell for now with your smile and with your eyes, indicating your confidence in your younger self. Perhaps you leave a gift, a token to remind her of her unchanging worth…a reminder of your abiding love and concern. Perhaps you tell her you will visit her very often. The child smiles at that thought as she ponders the many learning experiences that lie ahead… and the many happy moments to come. Sense her body softening and relaxing, and her chin lifting. What is it like for the child to realize now that she is not alone? That at least one person loves and cares for her? That she can ask for help? And you know that you have made a valuable visit. Your love has mattered. It has made a difference. Track your body and emotions as you ponder this.

Track Your Results

Repeat this exercise at least three times, on three consecutive days. You can choose to focus on the same event or time or on other distressing times. Repetition increases the benefits. Record your experience in your Skills Record (see appendix A).

Getting to the Bottom of Things: Floatback Strategies

Floating Back for Disturbing Events

Have you ever experienced an event that triggered strong negative emotions that seemed excessive? Perhaps you overreacted with anger, fear, or sadness and wondered, "Why am I so upset? Where is this coming from?" ACEs provide a clue to the mystery, for we understand now that old memories get locked in the brain with the original emotions. Recent events that stir similar emotions can pull up aspects of an old memory, including the original emotions. These old emotions can then drive our reactions in the present.

Usually we can tell when our strong emotions are getting in the way of our lives. They might be hurting our present functioning, our relationships, or our emotional well-being. We can use awareness of these strong emotions to our benefit by using what's called the *floatback* strategy.

The floatback strategy was originated by William Zangwill, further developed and named by Cindy Browning (1999), and popularized by Francine Shapiro (2012). The strategy helps soothe both the recent event and the old memory that is driving your emotional reaction to the recent event. You will actually be rewiring your brain so as to experience the new and old events—and yourself—in a more positive way.

We'll call the old event that is locked in memory the *core memory*, because it is stored in the deeper parts of the brain and fuels present reactions. Let's see how the core memory is linked to the present, and explore how that link can be broken by looking at Isaac's story. Notice the two major parts of the floatback strategy: 1) identify and soothe the recent event, and 2) identify and soothe the core memory.

Isaac's Story

Isaac admires calm people, and he tries to be reasonable and calm in his dealings at home and at work. To supplement his income, he moonlights as a writer for a local newspaper, working at home after his regular job. When his computer freezes when he is working at home, he becomes inordinately angry, so much so that he pounds his desk in rage and frustration. His head feels hot, like it is about to explode, and his stomach feels like it is tied in knots. He feels foolish, because he knows he is overreacting, yet he doesn't understand why he reacts so strongly to what seems like less than a life-or-death setback.

Isaac tried the floatback strategy for this event. First, he made a space to mindfully ponder the recent event. He noticed that in addition to his anger, he was feeling powerless, helpless, and alone. He even felt some fear and feelings of inadequacy. This was quite a revelation. He was able to soothe these reactions. Then he traced back to an early memory where he also experienced these feelings. He recalled the day his dad walked out and left the family. Isaac had prayed that his parents would stay together. He had worked hard around the house, been conscientious in school, and tried to be responsible, hoping to keep them happy and together. When his father left, he felt powerless, helpless, and alone. He was angry at his dad, worried for the welfare of his family, and doubting his ability to take care of the family members left at home. All of this made so much sense now. After Isaac soothed this core memory with the floatback strategy, he found that he reacted far less intensely to the computer glitches.

Table 13.1 is the written record of Isaac's floatback strategy, broken down into the two major parts: 1) identify and soothe the recent disturbing event, and 2) identify and soothe the core memory. Let's see how this floatback strategy works.

Table 13.1: Isaac's Floatback Strategy for Disturbing Events

	Recent Disturbing Event	Core Memory
Brief Description of Event (including age)	Computer freezes when I'm working alone at night; I'm 48 years old	Dad leaves when I'm 14 years old
Emotions	Angry, afraid, helpless, powerless, lonely	Angry, afraid, helpless, powerless, lonely, frustrated
Bodily Sensations	Head feels like it's about to explode; flushed face; tight jaw and chest; stomach in knot	Crushed, weighed down, heavy, slumped posture, tense muscles
Images	Isolated and alone, like the day I found out Dad was leaving	Sitting in Dad's chair, sad and alone
Thoughts	I'm alone and powerless to fix this. Things aren't working as they should.	I am powerless to keep Mom and Dad together. Things aren't going as they should in our family.
SUDs Rating Before Floatback Exercise	8	9
SUDs Rating After Floatback Exercise	4	3

Identify and Soothe the Recent Event

The center column in Isaac's chart describes the recent disturbing event and the associated reactions—emotions, bodily sensations, images, and thoughts. Recall the principle of reconsolidation: when we bring the aspects of a memory to conscious awareness, the brain has a chance to modify the memory. In the last two rows, Isaac rated the Subjective Units of Distress Scale (SUDS) at an 8. SUDS ratings range from 0 to 10, where 10 is the most distressing level of stress imaginable, 0 is no distress at all, and 5 is moderate distress. The SUDS rating helps gauge progress. Isaac soothed the recent event, then rerated the SUDS level at 4.

Identify and Soothe the Core Memory

After floating back to the core memory, Isaac filled in the third column. The initial SUDS rating of 9 was entered in the second-to-last row. After soothing the core memory, Isaac rerated the SUDS level as 3. Any drop in SUDS ratings, however small, is significant.

The Floatback Strategy for Disturbing Events

Now you are ready to try the floatback strategy for your own disturbing events. Prepare for this strategy by identifying a recent disturbing event that you'd like to trace back to a core memory. Shapiro (2012, 94) notes that most people have ten to twenty core memories that are "running [their] show"—causing emotional overreactions. These events are not always severe traumas, but overreaction is generally caused by an unprocessed memory.

Perhaps you get more upset than others around you do over a similar situation. For example, if you had a harshly critical father, you may get triggered and feel strong emotions of inadequacy and anger whenever someone else in authority or in your family uses a similar tone of voice or facial expression. Perhaps other people have even told you that you are overly sensitive or that you overreacted in a certain situation. This, of course, rarely helps, but floatback strategies often do. Try this floatback strategy if recalling a core memory isn't too distressing and if soothing the recent disturbance results in a drop in the SUDS rating. Test the waters with some caution to avoid being overwhelmed. Start by working with a recent event that is only moderately distressing before deciding to try this with a more distressing recent event.

Shapiro (2012) advises that if willpower and your normal problem-solving efforts—gathering information, tackling the problem, seeking assistance—haven't helped, suspect a stuck, unprocessed, negative memory. Shapiro also advises that this technique not be tried for complex traumatic memories or if you are in treatment for such. If you are concerned that a traumatic memory might be overwhelming, seek the aid of a trauma therapist. A skilled trauma therapist can use very effective trauma-processing skills such as EMDR to assist you in uncovering and settling core memories.

Don't be concerned if all your reactions are not clear at this time. For example, you might not recall the facial expression (image) of an offending person or all of your emotions. These might become clearer later.

Instructions

You can use the blank worksheet on page 103 or download one at http://www.newharbinger.com/46646. Sit comfortably in a place where you will not be disturbed for about thirty minutes. Relax your body. Focus on your breath for a few moments until your breathing becomes slow and regular.

IDENTIFY AND SOOTHE THE RECENT EVENT

1. Identify a recent event that stirred up *moderately* disturbing emotions—perhaps a 4 or 5 SUDS rating.

2. With a soft and open heart, hold this incident in full awareness. Without judging your reactions in any way, simply notice the reactions that this event evokes—emotions, bodily sensations, images, and then thoughts. Asking yourself, "What's the most disturbing part of this event?" might help you identify your reactions more clearly. Remind yourself, "Whatever I feel is okay. Let me feel it."

3. Pause to write down the facts surrounding the event in the middle column of the blank chart (putting distress into words calms the amygdala, a key structure in the brain that regulates emotions). Then record the emotions, sensations, images, and thoughts. When that is completed, record an initial SUDS rating.

4. Relax again. Focus on your breathing for a few moments.

5. Thinking again about the recent event and your reactions, sit mindfully with all the reactions. Let the emotions, sensations, images, and thoughts come to awareness again. Soften your body and hold your reactions with compassion. Especially notice where your body holds the disturbance. Now soothe these reactions. Breathe into and out from that area with deep compassion, loving-kindness, and acceptance. Whatever it is, let yourself feel it.

6. Repeat silently or aloud the self-compassion statements: "This is a moment of suffering; suffering is part of life; may I be kind to myself in this moment; may I give myself the compassion I need" (Neff 2011), as you did in chapter 6. Notice how this feels in your body.

7. When you are ready, take a more intentional in-breath, breathing into the area that has been holding the upset. On the out-breath, let awareness of that region of the body dissolve. The feeling of loving-kindness remains in your heart, as you repeat: "May I be happy, may I be at ease, may I be whole."

8. Think about your SUDS rating now. Write down the new SUDS rating in the last row of the chart. If the distress has by now subsided somewhat, it is probably safe to continue. (If not, it might indicate an old memory that needs to be processed with the help of a mental health professional.)

IDENTIFY AND SOOTHE THE CORE MEMORY

1. Now, recalling the recent event and your original reactions, let your mind float back to your childhood and notice an earlier time that comes to mind when you felt the same way. This might be the earliest memory, the worst memory, or just one that you remember from earlier years.

2. As you did before, notice the old event—the facts and your reactions: emotions, sensations, images, and thoughts. There is no judgment, just a curious interest and acceptance of what occurred at that time.

3. Record in the third column the facts (including your age at the time of the event), your reactions, and the initial SUDS rating. Reflect on how the old memory is influencing your life today.

4. Now soothe the old memory. Noticing where in your body you are holding the upsetting feelings, breathe compassion and loving-kindness into that area(s) on the in-breath. On the out-breath, let compassion settle there. Continue to focus on this area and your breathing as you notice what happens. Think to yourself, "Whatever; I feel is okay. Let me feel it." Remind yourself, "This is just an old memory, old stuff. It's all right; just continue to breathe loving-kindness into the area holding the disturbance."

5. Repeat silently or aloud the self-compassion statements: "This is a moment of suffering; suffering is part of life; may I be kind to myself in this moment; may I give myself the compassion I need" (Neff 2011), as you did in the first part of this exercise. Continue mindfully breathing compassion into the areas of your body and repeating the self-compassion statements. Notice how that feels in your body. Notice if any of your reactions have shifted somewhat.

6. If you wish, continue to soothe your reactions to the core memory in any way that seems helpful. You might use any of your favorite tools, such as:

   • The skills to regulate stress arousal that you practiced in chapter 5. These skills include the five-minute foot-to-head stress reducer or the body-based skills (knead, ground in your body, resistance, or change posture).

   • The emotional freedom technique (EFT) or the pass-through technique that you practiced in chapter 6.

   • You might also think of embracing that younger child until the pain subsides and good feelings return. Perhaps you provide the younger child with needed assurances, such as, "You are not alone. You will get through this and smile again."

7. When you are ready, take a more intentional in-breath, and on the out-breath, let awareness of the area holding the pain dissolve. Let your face soften into a satisfied, contented half-smile, as you realize you have gotten through that difficult time.

8. Notice now how you are feeling. What are you sensing in your body? Has anything shifted—your breathing, heartbeat, muscle tension, temperature, sensations in your gut? Have your emotions shifted? Images? Thoughts? Rerate your SUDS level as you now think about the core memory.

Floatback Strategy for Disturbing Events

	Recent Disturbing Event	Core Memory
Brief Description of Event (including age)		
Emotions		
Bodily Sensations		
Images		
Thoughts		
SUDS Rating Before Floatback Exercise		
SUDS Rating After Floatback Exercise		

Track Your Results

You'll likely find that this skill becomes more effective with repetition, so practice this strategy on each of three consecutive days to gain confidence. Make entries in your Skills Record (see appendix A).

As the brain rewires in constructive ways, you might notice additional positive shifts in your reactions to old or recent events. Pay attention to this.

Remember to practice the skills you learned in chapters 5 and 6 to soothe any disturbance that arises in connection to old or recent events. You might try self-compassion, body-based techniques, EFT, and the pass-through technique.

If you have difficulty soothing the old memory, perhaps it is not sufficiently processed. This might signal a need for the help of a trauma specialist. You might imagine putting the memory in a container and putting it into a freezer chest until you are ready to "unthaw" the memory with a therapist's assistance.

CHAPTER 14

Floating Back to Core Beliefs

Locked inside old memories that continue to play out in your present life are *core beliefs*. Core beliefs are deeply held beliefs about yourself that are embedded in the early years. We hardly notice them—and may not even put them into words, so they are rarely challenged or modified and continue to affect the way we experience ourselves.

In this floatback strategy, you'll start by bringing to awareness powerful negative beliefs that you hold about yourself and trace them back to their origin. Then you'll soothe and replace them.

The Six Basic Needs

Each person needs to satisfy six basic needs in order for self-esteem and emotional well-being to flourish. Each of us needs to *think* and *feel* and *sense*:

- **I am worthwhile.** Although individuals can differ in *market* or *social* worth, *human* worth is unconditional, infinite, equal, and unchanging. Unconditional human worth is a gift that comes with birth. This worth is not changed by mistakes, faults, or mistreatment by others. Neither is it affected, for bad or good, by externals, such as wealth, looks, education, relationship status, or health.

- **I am loving and lovable.** Love provides the security for our growth and exploration. It powerfully affects our brain and biology in a host of beneficial ways.

- **I am generally adequate.** No one is perfect or skilled in all areas. In fact, it is normal to feel inadequate at times and in certain situations. But healthy people believe that they are generally capable of living well and meeting life's challenges reasonably well.

- **I can grow and pick myself up after mistakes.** The person with wholesome self-esteem understands that worth is not jeopardized by mistakes, falling short of goals, or other setbacks. These don't define you. People with self-esteem believe that as they persist, they will get better at meeting life's challenges, becoming better and happier individuals. In short, they keep hope alive.

- **I am basically good.** *Good* in this sense refers to good character. There is no abiding sense of inner contentment and self-respect for those who have a bad reputation with themselves. Good character does not mean perfection. Rather, it means that we are trying our best and are on a good course.

- **I am safe.** Healthy people see the world as reasonably predictable, people as generally trustworthy, and themselves as being able to find their way in the world.

Ponder how ACEs disrupt these basic needs, leading to painful, negative core beliefs taking root and damaging self-esteem. These negative core beliefs are common to depression, anxiety, anger, and many other stress-related conditions. Table 14.1 suggests some ways that ACEs can lead to negative core beliefs (suggested by Shapiro 2012).

Table 14.1: How ACEs Impact Core Beliefs

Adverse Childhood Experience	Can Lead to Negative Core Beliefs Like These
Left alone, neglected	I don't matter. I'm not lovable.
Critical, overcontrolling parent	I'm not good enough. I'm inadequate. I can't win anyone's love or approval.
Abusive caregiver	I'm worthless; I was treated like garbage—I must be garbage. I must be bad. I can't stop this abuse. I'm powerless, helpless. I'm not safe. I can't trust people.
Parents' divorce	I'll repeat their mistakes; I can't be different. I'm hopeless. People I love will leave me. I'm not lovable.*
Made fun of by others at school	I'm different; I'm worthless.
Hearing parents argue	It's not safe; bad things will happen.

---

* *Note:* Fear of abandonment is common in those with panic disorder, most of whom experienced separation from a parent (Shapiro 2012).

Damaged self-esteem makes perfect sense when you understand the events you've experienced and how you reacted to those events. Fortunately, we can change the brain's wiring associated with these old beliefs.

Floatback to Core Beliefs Strategy

This strategy follows a process similar to the one you practiced in the previous chapter. However, the object is to trace back to, and rewire, specific damaging beliefs.

Instructions

1. The following chart lists beliefs that people have, grouped according to the six basic needs. The first column lists common *negative* beliefs acquired by people. Slowly scan them, placing a check beside those that you experience and are disturbing. *Common* implies that you are not alone in experiencing these. There is nothing unusual about having them; they are understandable. They are acquired through negative experiences with caregivers, siblings, peers, the media, and so on— and they can be changed. (The second column is a sampling of positive beliefs that can, with practice, replace the negative beliefs.) Awareness is the first step to uprooting and replacing your negative thoughts. A copy of this worksheet is also available at http://www.newharbinger.com /46646.

Core Beliefs

✓	Negative Beliefs	Positive Beliefs
	Worthwhile as a Person	
	I'm worthless.	I'm worth*while*...worth the *while* needed to grow.
	I don't matter.	Everyone matters. Each person has potential. "Even my little dance matters."
	I'm insignificant, unimportant.	I'm a worthwhile person.
	I'm different.	I'm unique and worthwhile.
	I'll never get X's approval.	Even if I don't have X's approval, I can love, accept, and approve of myself.

✓	Negative Beliefs	Positive Beliefs
	Loving and Lovable	
	I'm not lovable.	I am lovable.
	I can't love.	I am learning to love.
	I'm ugly.	My imperfect body is a miracle to appreciate.
	No one will love me as I am.	Maybe someone will love me as I am. In the meantime, I choose to love myself.
	Generally Adequate	
	I'm incompetent, inadequate, powerless, out of control, weak.	I'm imperfect and improving. Sometimes I don't have total control; that's okay! I'm certainly good at some things. Imperfect people are still worthwhile. Weakness can be changed to strength. I am stronger now.
	I'm stupid, an idiot.	I'm progressing. I'm just like other people. I have some strengths; other areas could use work.
	I can't do anything.	I can do some things. I certainly do some things well and will learn to do many more things well.
	I can't get from life what I want.	I think I can get what I want. I have choices now.
	I'm defective.	Who doesn't have defects? I'm still worthwhile.
	I can't handle this.	I will handle this, even though it's unpleasant.
	I'm damaged.	My core is intact.

✓	Negative Beliefs	Positive Beliefs
	Growth After Mistakes	
	I'm a failure.	I'm imperfect and full of potential.
		I can succeed.
		My mistakes don't define me.
		I am more than my mistakes.
	I must be perfect.	I'm sufficient.
		I choose to try to do a good, even excellent job.
	I must be 100 percent successful.	It's okay to make mistakes as I learn.
		Where is it written that I must bat 1000?
		I'm successful when I try my best and am learning.
	I'm hopeless.	Where there's life, there is hope.
		I will learn from this.
		I keep my dreams alive.
	Personal Goodness	
	I'm a bad person.	I'm trying to be good.
		I desire to be good.
		I learn from my mistakes.
	I'm a terrible person.	I'm imperfect *and* worthwhile.
	I'm shameful.	I make mistakes, just like everyone else; too bad.
	Safety and Trust	
	I can't trust anyone.	Some people are trustworthy.
		Some people are partially trustworthy.
		I can choose to trust some people.
	I can't show my feelings.	I trust my feelings.
	I'm in danger.	I was in danger. Now I'm safe.

2. Select a negative belief you'd like to change. Write it down in the first box on the left on the work-sheet on page 112. (A copy of this worksheet is also available at http://www.newharbinger.com /46646.)

3. Pause for a few moments. Relax your body as completely as possible. Focus on your breathing, watching your belly rise and fall with each breath.

4. Bring the negative belief that you selected into *full* awareness, without trying to fight or change it. As you continue to breathe and relax, just curiously notice without judging what you experience as you hold that belief in your mind. What feeling (or feelings) does that belief elicit? Where do you sense the upset in your body? For example, do you notice a change in your breathing or heart rate, muscle tension, or sensations in your gut, chest, throat, or head? Hold all of that in mindful awareness—with curious interest and compassion. If you wish, soothe your body with mindful breathing and self-compassion statements: "This is a moment of suffering; suffering is part of life; may I be kind to myself in this moment; may I give myself the compassion I need" (Neff 2011).

5. Float back to the core memory—an event in your early years when you feel that belief may have first occurred. If you can't identify an earlier event, just float back to an earlier time in your life when you felt that feeling and thought that thought. Without judging, notice the emotions and sensations stirred up by the core belief. What images do you remember of the event? What did you look like at the time? Notice your posture, facial expression, gestures, and so forth. Fill out the remainder of the left side of the worksheet, including your age (in the core memory description) and the initial SUDS rating.

6. When you've finished filling in the left column in the worksheet, sit in mindful awareness with all that you have written. Breathe compassion into the area(s) of your body holding the disturbance. Remind yourself, "This is just an old memory. Whatever I feel is okay; let me feel it." Soothe the memory. Repeat silently or aloud self-compassion statements: "This is a moment of suffering; suffering is part of life; may I be kind to myself in this moment; may I give myself the compassion I need" (Neff 2011). Continue to mindfully breathe compassion into the areas of your body that hold the disturbance and repeat the self-compassion statements. Notice how that feels in your body. Notice if any of your reactions have shifted somewhat.

7. Fill out the right side of the worksheet by writing down a positive replacement belief(s). Hold that belief in focused awareness. Repeat it silently three times as you let that belief settle in your body. Breathe calmly. Notice where that belief affects your body. Imagine that part of your body is just holding that thought. Notice how that makes your body feel.

8. Sit mindfully, curious as to the process that is unfolding. Enjoy the feelings and sensations in your body. Imagine yourself back then really internalizing this new belief. See your chin lift, your spine

straighten, and your face show a contented, confident expression. Your body moves fluidly, with a bounce in your step. You might also change the scene in any other way that you wish.

9.   Say silently as you relax your body, "This is a moment of peace. May I be happy. May I feel at ease."

10.   Track what has happened in your body. Has there been a shift in your bodily sensations, such as a reduction in tightness anywhere, a more relaxed posture, and so on? Have there been any shifts in your emotions?

11.   Complete the remainder of the right column on the worksheet, including the new SUDS rating as you consider the original core belief.

Core Belief Record

Negative Belief About Yourself	Positive Belief (Replacement Thought)
Core Memory (Describe)	
Emotions	New Emotions
Unpleasant Sensations in Body	New Bodily Sensations
Images (especially of self)	New Images (especially of self)
Initial SUDS Rating	New SUDS Rating

Track Your Results

Repeat this process for each negative belief you'd like to work with. Repetition helps the brain rewire and ingrain the new thought patterns.

As you've done in the past, record your experiences in your Skills Record (see appendix A). If you wish, remember to use any other skills from chapters 5 and 6 to regulate physical or emotional arousal, including body-based strategies, the tapping technique, and the pass-through technique. You might also imagine embracing that younger self until the pain subsides and good feelings return. Perhaps you provide the younger self with needed assurances or encouragement, such as, "It's understandable that you felt as you did. You are not alone. You will get past this and smile again."

As with other skills in this workbook, don't overdo it: as a general rule, don't practice this skill more than once a day. Take a break of a day or two if practicing this skill is distressing. Don't force yourself if it is not effective, and remember the option of seeking professional help for old memories that seem overwhelming.

Reworking Shame

CHAPTER 15

Shame and Self-Esteem

I introduced the concept of shame in chapter 3. In the context of ACEs, self-esteem and shame are closely intertwined. Let's consider some key principles related to self-esteem, shame, and ACEs:

- Self-esteem is damaged by ACEs and needs to be restored for healthy living.

- Damaged self-esteem is found in many stress-related psychological conditions, such as PTSD, depression, anxiety, addictions, alcohol abuse, and risky sexual behaviors.

- Sound self-esteem is linked to resilience and associated with better recovery following exposure to traumatic events.

- Shame is the opposite of healthy self-esteem. Low self-esteem and shame have intense self-dislike in common.

- Shame is experiencing the core self as damaged and defective. Like low self-esteem, shame is often implicitly experienced. It is the felt sense of disgust, self-contempt, or self-loathing.

- Shame programming disrupts fulfillment of the six basic needs of emotional well-being described in chapter 14.

The origins of shame are no mystery. Shame can occur at any time in life, and can result predictably from ACEs that often lead to spoken or unspoken conclusions, as shown in Table 15.1. The wounds caused by such events are particularly damaging when the events occur in the early years. And distressing present events can draw you back in time to the original shaming.

Table 15.1: ACEs and Shame-Based Thinking

ACE	Conclusions (conscious or unconscious)
Parents' divorce	My parent wouldn't have abandoned me if I was lovable. I'm to blame for bad things that happen.
Critical, overcontrolling, overprotective parents	I'm inadequate.
Parents' rage	I can't please people or be loved.
Parents are bad	I'm their offspring, so I must be bad, too.
Mother's look of disgust or boredom as she changes diapers, rather than smiling or being playful	I don't matter. I'm not valued. I'm disgusting.
Abuser told you, "Don't tell anyone, or else."	My secrets make me shameful, different. I'm powerless to protect myself.
Abuser gave you false message that you are bad, seductive, or trash beside the road.	I'm no good, damaged.

When I think of the imprint of shame, I think of Maria. Maria was an aerobics instructor—beautiful, fit, and intelligent. Maria had been hospitalized three times for anorexia, an eating disorder, in a nationally recognized program. That program focused simply on changing eating behavior, rather than modifying deeply rooted shame. Maria was filled with shame. She thought she was fat, ugly, and inadequate. Maria's parents had a troubled marriage. Her mother was anxious and detached. Her father was critical and withheld his love and approval. When she reached puberty, her mother told her to ask her father for permission to wear a bra. He said sarcastically, "What do you need a bra for?" To add to her shame, Maria was precociously developing, and the boys at school teased her for being "too fat." Ironically, but understandably, Maria's shame prevented her from experiencing herself in a positive light.

An important part of recovering from ACEs and cultivating self-esteem is neutralizing shame. It is difficult to heal shame with standard cognitive approaches because shame plays out primarily at the felt-sense level. A basic healing principle is that the core self survives and is worthwhile, lovable, and capable of growing, even though shame programming says the opposite. You might view shame as a call to love and accept your imperfect core self, a self that might have been mistreated.

Love is the healing agent and a strong countermeasure to shame. Recall that love releases oxytocin in the brain. Oxytocin reduces cortisol and calms and buffers stress. Love helps rewire neural shame circuitry, overwriting it with self-liking. In the next eight chapters, we'll be utilizing the reconsolidation principle to re-pair shaming memories with loving, compassionate memories. The goal is to replace shame and self-criticism with self-liking, compassion, and acceptance, methodically replacing old programming with new neural circuitry.

ACEs Model

We might depict the relationships between ACEs , self-esteem, shame, and health outcomes as follows:

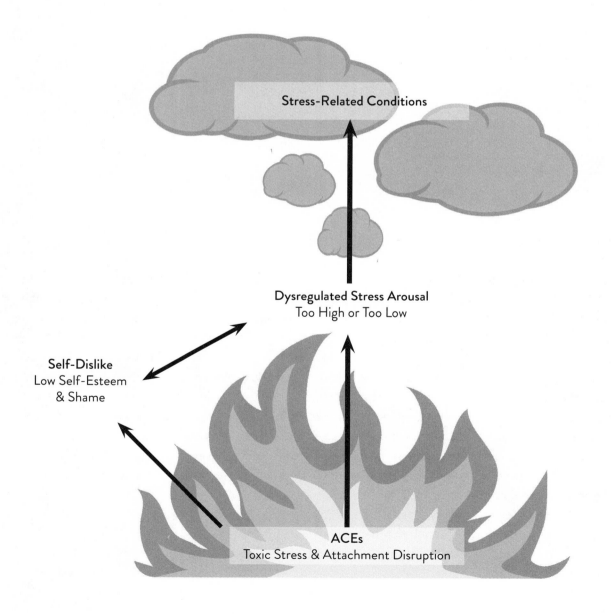

Stress-related conditions, both medical and psychological, range from depression, anxiety, and post-traumatic stress to pain and autoimmune disorders. As Felitti (2002) said, this is the smoke, not the flame. The flame is the toxic stress of **ACEs**, including attachment disruption. Unsettled ACEs lead to **dysregulated stress arousal**, including cortisol disruptions. Dysregulated stress—arousal that is stuck on too high or too low—puts us at greater risk for the stress-related conditions.

ACEs can lead directly to dysregulated stress arousal. Alternatively, ACEs can lead to **self-dislike**, which reciprocally interacts with dysregulated stress. For example, people lacking in self-esteem are more stressed by ego threats, secreting six times more cortisol (Kirschbaum et al. 1995). Dysregulated stress can in turn lower self-esteem.

This model suggests several intervention points to improve your well-being. For example, to get to the root of your suffering, you can settle the disturbing ACE memories, regulate physical and emotional arousal, and neutralize shame and low self-esteem (Eidhof et al. 2019). You have already learned how to regulate physical and emotional arousal, and you have begun to rewire the neural pathways related to early toxic memories. The next eight chapters will focus specifically on the important work of neutralizing shame.

Exploring Shame

Shame is so painful that it goes underground; we tend to block it from awareness. Yet unchallenged, shame continues to exert its influence on our lives, blocking healing and happiness. Changing shame starts with kind awareness—bringing it out of the shadows and soothing it with compassion. There is great benefit to simply practicing being aware of shame symptoms without judging them or reacting to them.

You might wish to turn to appendix B, "Shame Symptoms Inventory." With curious interest, and with a kind, nonjudgmental eye, simply check the signs and symptoms of shame that you experience. Do this with an open heart and a sense of optimism that you will eventually learn to experience yourself in positive new ways.

Rate Your Level of Shame

In order to calmly acknowledge the level of shame you are dealing with, fill out the following worksheet. A copy of this worksheet is also available at http://www.newharbinger.com/46646.

Rate your shame from 0 (none) to 10 (highest possible).

1. How much is shame interfering with your life?

    _____   *Not at all*

    _____   *A moderate amount*

    _____   *Greatly*

    _____   *Incapacitating*

2. Imagine that you woke up tomorrow and found that your shame rating had dropped. How would that feel in your body? Can you imagine anything that would enable that shame rating to drop?

    _____

    _____

    _____

    _____

    _____

    _____

CHAPTER 16

Rework Shame from Parents

This chapter guides you to rework shame messages and patterns that your parents may have knowingly or unknowingly imprinted in your brain. Remember to exercise caution throughout this chapter and this workbook: if this or any other exercise becomes too uncomfortable, put it aside or seek professional counseling.

Wolin and Wolin (1993) studied resilient children who coped well with difficult childhoods. They noted that these children could acknowledge problems that their parents struggled with, but were then able to create a healthy distance from their parents and pursue their own dreams. For example, a child might think, "Mom struggled with depression and trauma." Or, "Dad was an alcoholic who never learned how to have inner peace. He didn't respect himself, so he didn't respect others. I don't have to buy into his criticisms." These resilient children separated themselves from their parents figuratively ("I'm not my dad; I don't have to repeat his mistakes") and literally—perhaps moving some distance away to gain safety and the freedom to follow their own dreams.

Standing Up to Shame

In this exercise, you will confront shame in the best possible way, from a position of compassion and inner strength. As with other scripts in the workbook, you can read and apply these instructions one at a time, have someone read them to you, or record and then listen to them.

Instructions

1. Sit comfortably in a place where you will be undisturbed for about fifteen minutes. Rest, release, and relax in your breath. Let the gentle rhythm of your breath deeply relax your body as you let go of tension and any negative thoughts.

2. Imagine, if you can, a time early in life when you felt shame in the presence of a parent (or significant caregiver). Perhaps you were neglected or treated as though you had little value, and you

internalized negative messages about yourself. It's all right if you can't identify a specific memory. Remembering a general time frame will work for this exercise.

3. If you can, imagine the expression on your caregiver's face—perhaps a scowl or a look of disinterest or disgust. Perhaps upon looking more closely, you see fear, sadness, insecurity, or preoccupation. Whatever comes up is all right.

4. See you, the younger child, perhaps feeling shamed, anxious, or empty—thinking something is wrong with you, like you are not enough. With great compassion, notice what the child is experiencing—sensations in the body, emotions, images, and thoughts. No wonder you had these reactions! You were just a child.

5. Now imagine that you, the wise grown-up, comfort and protect the child in any way that is needed.

6. Then, from a safe distance, look into your caregiver's eyes with loving-kindness. View your caregiver's suffering with compassion. Acknowledge that your caregiver had problems. You know that, from a safe distance, you can view his or her suffering with some detachment and understanding.

7. Imagine saying, "I have a right to feel happy and whole." This is said not with anger or resentment, but with compassion for yourself, calm determination, and a sense of inner strength. Track how that feels in your body to declare that. Slowly push your arms out in front of you to establish a safe boundary. Again, declare, "I have a right to feel happy and whole." Track how that feels in your body.

8. Imagine saying the following, slowly tracking how it feels after each statement:

    I value myself.

    I take good care of myself.

    I'm quite strong and capable.

    I'm not my parent. I'm building a better life.

    I'm a transition person in my family.

Practice this exercise once daily over a three-day period before proceeding to the next exercise.

Rewiring Early Shame

This strategy overwrites general shame programming at many levels: bodily sensations, body movements, emotions, thoughts, images, and intentions. As with other scripts in the workbook, you can read and apply these instructions one at a time, have someone read them to you, or record and then listen to them.

Instructions

1. Think again about the shamed child in the early years. Bring compassion to that child. Start by noticing kindly and with curious interest how you experienced shame back then (Ogden and Fisher 2015):

   • Sensations of the external world (for example, sights, smells, taste, sounds, touch)

   • Sensation of your internal world (such as tingling, vibrating, trembling, shivering, dullness, dry throat, nausea, heaviness, feeling uptight, tightness in the chest or stomach, breathing difficulty, shallow breathing or other changes in breathing, loss of energy, pressure, congestion, pounding or racing heart, tension in jaw or elsewhere, feeling hollow)

   • Body movements (such as constricted or hunched posture—slumped spine, hiked shoulders, making yourself small, lowered head, sagging shoulders—changes in your facial expression, impulses to move, turning away, clenched jaw, furrowed brow, clenched fist, going limp, frozen gestures)

   • Emotions (such as sad, anxious, worried, angry)

   • Thoughts (for example, "Dad was a bad man. I'm his son; therefore, I'm bad.")

2. As you bring forth the various memory aspects of this shame-filled time, comfort yourself with some of the skills you've already learned to regulate emotions and physical stress arousal, such as kneading your arm, using self-compassion statements, and reassuring yourself: "This is just an old memory. I'm learning better ways to respond."

3. Now imagine experiencing the opposite of shame—interrupting the old shame patterns and creating new response patterns and neural pathways (Ogden and Fisher 2015). For that shameful period of time, imagine life without shame—experiencing new:

   • *Feelings*, such as hope, confidence, adventure, cheer, play, self-love and compassion, and inner gladness to be you.

   • *Sensations.* What would these new emotions feel like in your body? Your heart rate might be steadier and slower, your muscles relaxed, and so on.

   • *Images.* What would you look like? What would your posture be like? How would you be moving? How would you see the world? How would your facial expression appear—pleasant, relaxed, a twinkle in your eye?

   • *Thoughts.* (For example, "No matter what others do or say, I am a worthwhile person." "No matter what others do or say, I love myself." "I have the capacity to grow and lift up myself and others.")

4. Finish this exercise with kind thoughts. Meditating on self-compassion and loving-kindness inten-
    tions like those below have been found to counter shame, depression, and anxiety, while increasing
    self-esteem (see Kearney et al. 2013). Calm yourself with your breathing. Hold an image of yourself
    in mind as you wish yourself well. Repeat the following silently or aloud (Nakazawa 2015, 172):

    May I be filled with love and kindness.

    May I be safe and protected.

    May I love and be loved.

    May I be happy and contented.

    May I be healthy and strong.

    May my life unfold with ease.

5. Place your hands over your heart. Focus on the area around your heart and repeat the intentions
    above as you slowly breathe. Pause between each intention, allowing it to settle in your heart.

6. Create a sense of kind connection to others—knowing that you can extend compassion to
    others—by repeating aloud or silently:

    May those I associate with be filled with love and kindness.

    May those I associate with be safe and protected.

    May those I associate with love and be loved.

    May those I associate with be happy and contented.

    May those I associate with be healthy and strong.

    May their lives unfold with ease.

Track Your Results

In turn, practice each of these exercises daily for at least three days. Describe your experiences in your
Skills Record (see appendix A).

CHAPTER 17

Rework Later Shame Programming

Over the course of our lives, we all experience potentially shaming events—including ACEs, harsh criticism, insensitive teasing, or failing at something that seems very important. Events like these can ingrain very unpleasant shame programming in the brain. This chapter describes two strategies to change the shame programming for recalled time periods or events, typically occurring from years three to eighteen. In both of these strategies, you will apply the principles of reconsolidation to rewire consciously recalled memories.

Overriding Shame Programming with Thriving

This exercise, inspired by Ogden, Minton, and Pain (2006), provides a sense of perspective for an experience of shame that seems overwhelming. It helps you realize that shame programming is neither permanent nor taking over all aspects of your life. Through this exercise, thriving programming will come to replace the shame programming that is currently in the brain. As with other scripts in the workbook, you can read and apply these instructions one at a time, have someone read them to you, or record and then listen to them.

Instructions

1. **Identify a shame experience.** Recall a time when you felt overwhelmed, helpless, inadequate, embarrassed, inferior, disappointed in yourself, or humiliated. These are different distressing disguises for shame.

2. **Track shame**. Recall the benefits of simply tracking your reactions in your body. Track what you experience in your body. Simply notice without judging how you experience shame in your body. Where does the shame seem to be located? Does it have a size? Shape? Color? With compassion, breathe into that area holding the shame.

3. **Take perspective.** What part of your body *doesn't* feel that way? For example, you might notice a spot—perhaps above your breastbone or in an arm—that doesn't feel shame. Track that. This step reminds you that shame really isn't taking over every aspect of your being.

4. **Recall a triumph experience.** Think of a time when you felt safe, competent, successful, strong, capable, confident, or playful. For instance, you may want to think about a stroll in nature, being with good friends, or an accomplishment. Recall as many details as you can. Recall what you were doing, how your body was moving, and how your body felt inside. What emotions were you feeling? Recall the air on your skin, the sights, the sounds, or other sensations.

5. **Track the triumph experience.** As you think of this triumph experience, track what you experience in your body. How wonderful that you can feel that. You might sense yourself as strong and flexible. What else is going on inside your body? Is your spine rigid, or soft and flexible? What about your rib cage? You might notice a straightening of the spine, a lifting of the chin. Exaggerate these sensations and sense them deeply. Are your legs feeling strong? Relaxed? Is your body feeling energized? Is there a particular place in your body where you feel a sense of triumph…or pleasure? Track that. Track what is happening to your breathing as you recall your triumph experience.

6. **Assert your choice.** Stand tall, with your spine erect. Your muscles are relaxed and strong. You feel calm and confident. Realize that with practice, you can choose your focus and can override shame programming with thriving programming.

Practice this exercise three times over a three-day period before proceeding.

Exercise: Overwriting an Old Shame Scene

It is often said that we are as sick as our secrets. What do you think might happen if you were to write about shaming moments, putting on paper what you've perhaps never before disclosed but would have liked to? This is called expressive writing, which has repeatedly been found to improve health outcomes. For example, in one study, expressive writing worked as well as a well-established trauma treatment called cognitive processing therapy, with fewer dropouts (Sloan et al. 2018). Adding self-compassion statements to expressive writing can increase self-esteem, happiness, and self-soothing (Imrie and Troop 2012).

In expressive writing, you describe in writing the facts of the event, your feelings, and your thoughts about the event. Typically, you write for fifteen to thirty minutes for each of four days. If expressive writing is done with understanding and compassion, people often find that the difficult event loses its grip, and that the distress felt during the four days of writing is replaced by understanding, better mood and self-esteem, and better health. There seems to be a benefit to getting bottled-up feelings off your chest.

Once you have writing materials—a journal, sheets of paper, writing implements, or a computer—you are ready to begin this exercise, adapted from Kaufman (1996). Find a place where you won't be disturbed for fifteen to thirty minutes. Ideally, the place will be somewhere you won't make associations with the past, such as a table in the corner of a room.

Instructions

1. **Identify an old shame scene.** With curious interest, fully describe in writing the facts and details of the shaming event. Recall the principle of reconsolidation: bringing the aspects of a difficult memory to awareness affords the brain an opportunity to change the memory.

2. **Describe your reactions.** Write about the full range of feelings that you felt. Track what was happening in your body. You can add any insights that help you understand your feelings. You might also write about how that experience still influences you for good or bad, including how it has affected your present discomfort, relationships, lack of confidence, or feelings of self-contempt.

3. **Identify the source of the inner voice or felt sense of shame that persists today.** Was there a verbal message from someone? A facial expression? Write about that. What conclusion—about yourself, others, or the world—did you internalize from the experience? Write about that. Take your time.

4. **Direct self-compassion to yourself, as needed.** As you consider this old experience, you might knead your arm while quietly repeating, "This is a moment of suffering. Everyone suffers. May I bring compassion to this moment. May I give myself the compassion I need to heal."

5. **Create a new scene.** In writing, modify the old scene in any way you want. Describe the details of the new scene, and the new feelings, sensations, postures, inner voice, and self-compassion. It is okay to have new feelings of brightness, joy, belonging, confidence, safety from mistreatment, or freedom from excessive worry.

6. **Write a compassion letter to yourself.** Write as you would to your best friend or a beloved child. It is essential to include feelings. You might wish to express empathy and appreciation for what you have survived, the strengths you've shown, and the good you do—despite the difficult experiences you've endured. Take your time. Track what happens in your body as a result.

A Few Considerations to Keep in Mind

Write only for yourself. If you worry about someone seeing what you're writing, you might inhibit your expression. After you finish this exercise, you may wish to destroy your writing to protect your privacy.

You may choose to write about the same shaming event on each of the four days, or you might choose to write about different events. The choice is up to you.

Expect some difficulty during the four days of writing about an old shaming event(s). Typically, this is not too unpleasant, but after the four days of writing, your mood will likely lift above your pre-writing level. If writing about past shaming events becomes too difficult, ease up. You can write about a less distressing memory or seek the aid of a mental health professional.

Track Your Results

Practice each of these exercises in turn for three or four consecutive days, tracking your progress in your Skills Record (see appendix A).

CHAPTER 18

Soften Body Shame

Have you ever noticed what you see when you look in the mirror? Do you notice the imperfections with a sinking feeling? Or are you drawn with awesome wonder and gratitude to everything in your body that is working so well? Do you see past those physical imperfections and gladly behold the core person, the miracle that you are?

I recall Dan so well. Dan is a third-generation police officer who was paralyzed when he was shot by a drug dealer. He now navigates the world with his mechanized wheelchair. Dan's body is largely disabled, no longer lean and muscled. He could despise his body, but he doesn't. Instead, he appreciates what it can still do. Importantly, his mood is upbeat and his self-esteem is intact because he knows that his worth as a person is deeper than his imperfect body. He approaches each day with good humor, enthusiasm, and curiosity as to how he might be helpful to others.

How do you experience your body? How does the way you relate to your body affect your sense of self and your well-being?

Let's state some important principles. Your body is not your core, essential self. The core self is of infinite worth and unlimited potential. The body is an external, just like other externals, such as your income, marital status, or job title. Externals do not affect your core worth as a person. Thus, your body's changing appearance, chemistry, weight, energy level, or the way it's been treated do not affect your core worth—just as the fluctuating quality of other externals do not alter your unchanging worth as a person. It's not that things like adequate income, good appearance, and physical health are not desirable and worth pursuing. Rather, it is that we can more effectively pursue externals when we are secure about who we are inside.

Unfortunately, many people today equate self-esteem with their bodies. But self-esteem is an inner experience that is independent of externals.

So Where Do Shame and the Body Come In?

To a great degree, the body becomes the holder of shame, for we focus on, and experience, self-dislike there. This is particularly true if you were physically mistreated or if your body was ridiculed. However, any shaming emotion can play out in the body.

The body is a metaphor for the core self: how you experience your body is often similar to how you experience your core self. Experiencing your body with unpleasant feelings can reinforce shame circuits in your brain. Conversely, loving and appreciating your body registers in the right brain and helps rewire shame circuits.

The following exercise, adapted from Engle (2006), asks you to have a compassionate conversation with a disliked body part in a way that will change the way you experience that part. You can write in the blanks below, in a journal, on sheets of paper, or on a computer; or download a copy of the worksheet at http://www.newharbinger.com/46646.

A Conversation with a Shamed Body Part

To prepare to focus on your body, spend a few moments relaxing in your breath. Select a transition object that you can hold in your hand, such as a tennis ball. Focus on its texture and feel (Gilbert and Procter 2006).

1. Write about the part of your body you least like and why you feel that way. (For example, others made fun of a physical feature or you were very self-critical of that part.)

    _____

    _____

    _____

    _____

    _____

    _____

2. Breathe compassion into that part of your body, and track what is going on in your body as a whole. Take your time. Why do you appreciate, or have you appreciated that body part?

    _____

    _____

    _____

    _____

_____

_____

_____

3. If you were having a conversation with that part of your body, what would it say? What would it want you to know? Is there something it could teach you? Take your time to listen, and write down what comes up.

_____

_____

_____

_____

_____

_____

4. When you are finished, track your body and emotions. Notice if anything has shifted in a pleasant way. Describe it below.

_____

_____

_____

_____

This "conversation" can be very revealing and can change both the way we experience our bodies and ourselves, as evidenced in this example.

The Body Part's Message	What That Message Teaches Me
You made me feel bad because you don't accept me as I am.	I'll accept my body and treat it with gratitude and respect, not deflating harsh criticism. I'll take very good care of it. In the same way, I'll regard my core self with kind acceptance, which helps me grow better than harsh self-criticism or self-dislike does.
You only dwell on my imperfection, and miss what is right.	Whether it's my body or my core, noticing what is right is much more motivating than getting down about my flaws.
You are so much more than your imperfect body part.	I'm so much more than my rough edges and present weaknesses. I commit to enjoying my strengths, rather than dwelling on my weaknesses.
Despite my physical weakness, I've tried my best to serve you. I'd like you to appreciate what I've done for you.	Despite my inner weakness and challenges, I've made it this far. Hooray!

Track Your Results

Complete "A Conversation with a Shamed Body Part" exercise once each day for at least three days. You might converse with the same body part or try the exercise with different parts of your body. Describe your experience in your Skills Record (see appendix A).

CHAPTER 19

Loving the Body

The stress response tends to draw our attention to what's wrong and worrisome. This, of course, can be very useful in emergencies. With chronic stress, however, this focus can prevent us from experiencing the world—and our bodies—with wholesome pleasure. Toxic childhood stress from ACEs wires the brain to be chronically on alert, but brain plasticity affords us the opportunity to rewire the brain.

This chapter reinforces and builds upon the pattern started in chapter 18 of experiencing our bodies with kind awareness and appreciation. This new response is pleasant in its own right, but also changes shame wiring that helps keep the brain on high alert.

A moment's reflection convinces us that our bodies are truly miraculous. Think for a moment of the brain, which can execute more complex functions than any known computer. The heart, which tirelessly beats throughout our lifetime, and usually without problems, keeps blood pumping to all the cells in the body. Our ears and eyes are marvels of miniaturization, enabling us to hear a sleeping baby's breathing and appreciate the colors of a flower in spring. The skin and bones self-repair after injuries, while the complex immune system battles a host of harmful invaders.

Meditation: Loving the Body

Isn't it interesting that we often focus on our body's imperfections and fail to appreciate all that works so well—allowing us to enjoy the beauties of nature, feel a loved one's embrace, or feel the wind on our skin? This meditation, developed by mind/body master Joan Borysenko (1990, 220–223) and reprinted with permission, guides us to experience the body in a wholesome way, perhaps for the first time. The beneficial effects usually increase with repetition. Find a place to relax undisturbed for about twenty minutes. Then sit in the meditator's posture and prepare for a very pleasant experience. As with other scripts in the workbook, you can read and apply these instructions one at a time, have someone read them to you, or record and then listen to them.

Instructions

Take a deep breath and gently close your eyes. Give a few big sighs…sighs of relief…and see if your body wants to stretch a little…or yawn…(pause).

Now pay attention to the rhythm of your breathing…Feel your body rise gently as you breathe in, and relax as you breathe out…(pause for several breaths)…Every out-breath is an opportunity to let go…to feel the pleasant warmth and heaviness of your body…a little more on each out-breath…(pause).

Now, as you breathe in, imagine your breath as a stream of warm, loving light entering through the top of your head. Let it fill your forehead and eyes…your brain…your ears…and nose…Feel the light warm and relax your tongue, your jaws, and your throat. Let your whole head float in an ocean of warm light… growing brighter and brighter with each breath…(pause). Thank your eyes for the miracle of sight…your nose for the fragrance of roses and hot coffee on cold mornings (or whatever you like)…your ears for the richness that sound is…your tongue for the pleasure of taste…and let the light fill and heal every cell of your senses…

Breathe the light into your neck…let it expand gently into your shoulders…and breathe it down your arms…and into your hands…right to the tips of your fingers…Thank your arms and hands for all you have created and touched with your life…all the people you have hugged and held to your heart…Rest in the warmth and love of the light…light that grows brighter with every breath…

And breathe the warm light into your lungs and your heart…feeling it penetrate your entire chest, filling every organ, every cell with love. As you breathe, send gratitude to your lungs for bringing in the energy of life—and to your heart for sending life to all the cells of your body and for serving you so well for all these years…rest in the gratitude and love…in the light that continues to grow brighter with each breath…(pause).

And breathe the light into your belly, feeling it penetrate deeply into your center, into the organs of digestion and reproduction…and sense the miracle of your body…the mystery of procreation and of the ability to beget life…let the light expand through your torso and down into your buttocks…growing warmer and brighter…balancing and healing all the cells of your body…

Breathe the light into your thighs…into bone and muscle, nerve and skin, alive with the energy of light…comforted in your caring and your love…and let the light expand into your calves…and your feet… right to the soles of your feet…feeling gratitude for the gift of walking…letting the love-light grow brighter and brighter…

Rest in the fullness of the light…enjoying the life force…and, if there is any place in your body that needs to relax or to heal, direct the light there and hold that part of yourself with the same love you would give to a hurt child…(pause).

Now, as you breathe, sense how the light radiates out from your body…just as a light shines in the darkness, surrounding you in a cocoon of love…and you can sense that cocoon extending all around your body, above and below you, to all sides, for about three feet…like a giant cocoon…a place of complete safety where you can recharge your body and your mind…(pause).

And you can imagine the light around other people…surrounding them with the same radiance of love, gratitude, and healing…see your loved ones in the light…see those who you think of as your enemies in the light…Then let the light expand until you can imagine the entire world as an orb of light…(pause)… amidst a universe of light (pause)…all connected…all at peace…and feel the wonder and majesty of creation…(pause).

Now for a minute or two just rest…just breathe…returning to the warm, comfortable feelings within you…(long pause).

And now, begin to reorient yourself to the room…slowly and at your own pace…bringing the peace and gratitude back with you.

Track Your Results

Repeat this meditation so that you will have practiced it daily for at least three days. Describe your experience in your Skills Record (see appendix A).

CHAPTER 20

Healing Inner Dialogue

When stress arousal returns to the resilient zone—neither too high nor too low—areas of the brain that regulate logical thinking and verbalizing become active. The cognitive approach to healing can then help rewire shame circuitry in the brain. It does so by altering negative thought patterns, which with repetition alter your brain circuitry, emotions, and stress arousal.

Researchers and theorists have long recognized the effect of habitual thoughts on mental health. For example, a founding father of cognitive therapy, Aaron Beck, MD, identified what he called the depression triad, three thoughts commonly linked to depression. The three thoughts, in effect, are: "I'm no good," "I can't do anything," and "Things will never improve." In related research, Martin Seligman, one of the pioneers in positive psychology, identified the pessimistic attribution style. When asked to explain why a bad event happened and its impact on that person and their future, pessimists typically think that the event is:

- **Personal** ("Something is wrong with me at the core; I'm such a dummy.")

- **Pervasive** ("This is a consistent pattern in all areas; I mess up everything.")

- **Permanent** ("This is a stable, unchangeable pattern; things will never improve.")

Compared with optimistic thinkers, pessimists are less happy, experience poorer mental and physical health, are less professionally or athletically successful, and are less resistant to stress. In short, pessimists get bogged down in negativity—to their detriment.

Notice the parallels between the depression triad and the pessimistic style of thinking. Notice, also, that you can learn to replace negative thinking patterns with more upbeat thought patterns, such as those in the third column of the following chart.

	Depression Triad (Beck)	Pessimistic Attribution Style (Seligman)	Antidotes (Replacement Thoughts)
Self-condemnation	I'm no good.	Something is wrong with me at the core. I'm a loser. I'm dumb.	I am fallible, just like everyone else. This was a difficult, unfortunate *situation*. It doesn't define who I am. At the core, I am still worthwhile. I'm a worthwhile person.
Doubting Abilities	I can't do anything.	I mess up everything.	I can certainly do *some* things quite well.
Hopelessness	Things will never improve.	Things will never improve.	With experience and practice, I'll likely get better, slowly but surely. I can grow my strengths.

Depressing, pessimistic thoughts are really a shame setup. If left unchallenged, they can profoundly affect your well-being. For example, people suffer more PTSD symptoms when they view their trauma as defining who they are rather than viewing it as an unfortunate, unusual occurrence (an external; Foa et al. 1999). Conversely, replacing pessimistic thoughts with optimistic ones stimulates a brain region important to compassion, attachment, empathy, and peacefulness—while dampening areas related to emotional arousal (Newberg and Waldman 2009). So it is vitally important to overwrite negative thought patterns with upbeat ones.

Practicing the Healing Inner Dialogue

In the exercise that follows, you'll bring arousal levels within the resilience zone. Then you will mentally rehearse a kind, optimistic dialogue. With repetition, these thoughts will instill a new way of thinking, in effect helping to rewire shame circuits and replace them with compassion circuits. As with other scripts in the workbook, you can read and apply these instructions one at a time, have someone read them to you, or record and then listen to them.

Instructions

1. Find a place to relax undisturbed for about twenty minutes. Close your eyes, if that is comfortable.

2. Place your mind in your belly, as it were, and just pay attention to the natural rhythms of your breathing. Notice the rising and falling of your belly as you breathe. Take your time to settle in your breath.

3. Knead your arm, moving your hand up and down your forearm, in the way that feels best to you. Feel a sense of connection to your body. Track how that feels in your body.

4. Think of a time, a place, or an event that gave you a pleasant feeling. Perhaps this memory reminds you of an inner strength that you value. Recall this in as much detail as possible. Take your time. Track how this pleasant memory affects your body—your posture, what you sense. What emotions arise? It's okay to feel joy, confidence, peace, and the like.

5. Slowly repeat the first of the following statements three times with a kind, good-humored attitude. Take an easy, deep breath and allow time for it to settle into your mind and body. Repeat this for each statement, saying each with conviction and feeling. If you notice resistance to speaking kindly to yourself, accept that as fairly common at first. Patiently allow compassion to soften this resistance as you open your heart to the healing power of kindness.

    I feel composed and dignified because I am aware of my core worth.

    I am at peace with being imperfect—imperfect, yet infinitely perfectible.

    I am fallible. Everyone is. And that's okay.

    I have strengths and weaknesses. Everyone does.

    My mix of strengths and weaknesses is unique. I like being unique.

    I see myself as generally capable. I do some things quite well.

    Even though I'm imperfect, nevertheless I'm a worthwhile person.

    Even though I'm imperfect, nevertheless I enjoy trying and growing.

    Even though I make mistakes, nevertheless I love myself.

    Bad times don't define me. I am so much more than that.

    Being treated poorly does not change my core worth.

    Bad treatment strengthens my commitment to love myself.

    I'm inclined to think, "I can do this."

All in all, I'm doing pretty well.

Mistakes are externals, not who I am at the core.

I'll get better with experience.

I can laugh at the silly things I do sometimes.

I'll rise above adversity.

Things will turn out as well as possible if I do my part.

I find something to enjoy or appreciate each day, no matter what.

My life matters; I'm committed to making it count.

I open my heart to the love and friendship of good people.

I love my imperfect self and trust that at least some people will love me for who I am. If they don't, that's okay.

I love that I am gradually learning to love myself.

I'm not superhuman. It's okay to sometimes feel emotional pain.

I'm as worthwhile as anyone else, but no more. So I stay humble and inwardly secure.

I am quietly glad to be who I am.

6. When you've finished mentally rehearsing these statements, return your attention to your breathing. Track how your body feels now. Track your emotions. Do you notice any shifts, even subtle ones?

Track Your Results

Repeat this activity three times, once a day over a three-day period. Then fill out your Skills Record (see appendix A).

CHAPTER 21

Disconnect from Memory's Quicksand

Shameful memories are like quicksand, which pulls us in and keeps us stuck, even though we try so hard not to think about them. Steven Hayes, who originated acceptance and commitment therapy (ACT), has developed a very useful strategy called *defusing* for gaining emotional distance from chronic shameful memories that we've become fused with. Defusing is based upon four principles*:

1. **Nearly everyone suffers intense emotional pain sometimes.** Nearly all of us experience shame, sadness, or anxiety at times. According to Hayes, 90 percent of people will even have thoughts of suicide at some point in their lives. In other words, pain is a normal part of life.

2. **Most suffering results from the endless battles that we fight against our histories.** We get locked, or fused, in a battle against our painful memories, desperately trying to fix, solve, or erase the memories with thinking (self-talk). Say someone recently treated you harshly and made you feel inadequate. Perhaps this stirs up shame that is rooted in early life stress. You might think, "I hate this feeling. It's humiliating. I can't tell anyone I feel this way. What if I really *am* inadequate? I don't want to live with that feeling. I'll do something so adequate that I'll no longer feel inadequate. But what if I fail? Then I'll feel even more inadequate. I don't want to think about it. I'll find something to distract myself so I won't think about it." And the battle goes on and on—a battle that we can't win. Even the word "inadequate" is enough to throw you back into the battle and dredge up the old pain. We say that the word—in this case, "inadequate"—has become fused with the memory.

3. **Although we can control 95 percent of our outer problems (leaky faucets, flat tires, bad hair), we cannot get rid of our histories—the memories and painful feelings.** Thinking about a memory doesn't eliminate it, nor does trying *not* to think about it. Test this by thinking in detail about a chocolate cupcake. Visualize it. Smell it. Taste it. Feel it in your mouth. Now try not to think about it. After all, it adds lots of empty calories, so it would be good not to think about it. Of course, you will now think about it. You might even count how many times you think about it

---

* This section is adapted mainly from *Get Out of Your Mind and Into Your Life: The New Acceptance and Commitment Therapy* (Hayes and Smith 2005) and *ACT: An Experiential Approach to Behavior Change* (Hayes and Strosahl with Wilson 1999).

over the course of the next minute. It works the same way with a painful memory. Once you experience intense emotion, it is unlikely that "not thinking about it" will work. In fact, the more you try not to think about it, the more you will think about it. Memories can't simply be erased. Ironically, the more we fight against the memories, the more emotional charge they absorb. For respite, we might try to escape the battlefield. We try to run from the memory by trying not to think about it. Or we try to distract ourselves with sleep, working, shopping, sex, gambling, TV, painkillers, or other attempts to numb the pain. However, the memories return because they haven't changed.

4.   **Words pull us into the struggle.** Perhaps only thinking about the word "inadequate" (or "incompetent," "loser," "failure," or some other shaming word) draws us into the battle.

Diagrammed, the cycle of chronic emotional pain looks like this:

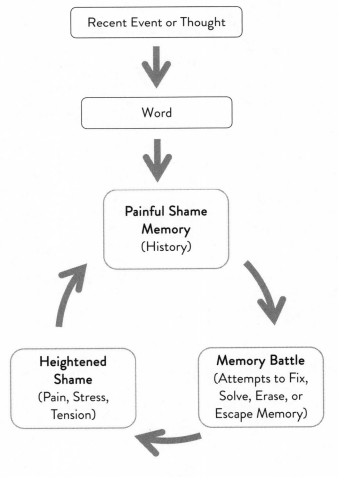

Figure 21.1: The Shame Cycle

A recent event, such as being criticized, or even a fleeting negative thought, triggers a shaming word, such as "inadequate." That word pulls you into the circular battle, stirring the pain of a shame memory. The natural tendency is to brace ourselves and fight the pain. However, this is a battle we can't win because we can't change a part of our history. The unsuccessful struggle only heightens shame's pain—keeping it in focus and increasing physical and emotional arousal. Heightened shame causes the brain to recall more shameful feelings and memories. This is called state-dependent memory retrieval. And the cycle continues.

What is required is a change in tactics! Paradoxically, we can better defuse or separate from the battle by fully joining the battle. That is, we can learn to fully let the pain into awareness with a completely accepting, welcoming, kind, and dispassionate attitude. We tend to the casualties, and then we step away from the battlefield and move on with our lives, without wasting energy trying to change the memory. This is the essence of the defusing technique. A worksheet for practicing this technique follows. A copy of this worksheet is also available at http://www.newharbinger.com/46646.

The Defusing Technique

1. Identify a moderately painful memory. Perhaps you'll recall a situation that made you feel embarrassed, rejected, shamed, disrespected, abused, ridiculed, inadequate, or unloved. Perhaps you made a mistake or a bad decision. Perhaps you were mistreated. Maybe a parent or "friend" labeled you lazy or a coward, and you've tried to run from that memory for years. Maybe you experienced adversity more recently. Briefly describe it below.

    _____

    _____

    _____

    _____

2. Write down how that situation bothered you. Describe the thoughts, feelings, images, and bodily sensations.

    Thoughts

    _____

    _____

    Feelings

    _____

    _____

Images

_____

_____

Sensations

_____

_____

3. How long has the memory bothered you? _____

    Has thinking gotten rid of it? _____

The Milk Exercise: A Small Detour

This activity demonstrates why the defusing technique works. Try this before proceeding:

A. Think about milk. Fully experience it in your mind and body. See what that word pulls up. Do you think of something white in a big glass? In a bottle? On cereal? Do you feel it coating your mouth, feeling cold and creamy? Do you hear "glug, glug" as you swallow, and feel it going down into your stomach? Does that feel good? Do you think, "I like the taste of milk," or "I'm lactose intolerant" or "Mom put milk on my cereal"? Just see what comes up. Isn't it interesting what a single word can trigger?

B. With neutral, nonjudgmental awareness, say the word "milk" aloud as fast as you can for forty-five seconds. (Pause.) When you have finished repeating the word "milk" for forty-five seconds, notice what happens. People often say that the way they experience the word "milk" changes. "Milk" just becomes a sound, without the meaning or sensations connected to the memory of milk.

In like fashion, repeating a word that is fused with a shameful memory tends to neutralize the word and the associated reactions of shame. Now you are ready to return to your worksheet and complete the defusing technique.

4. Thinking about your moderately painful memory, pick a single word that describes what the memory makes you feel about yourself—a word that goes to the heart of your pain. The word might be "bad," "inept," "dumb," "loser," "helpless," "powerless," "inadequate," "coward," "lazy," "disgusting," "shamed," "guilty," "stupid," "clumsy," and so on. Maybe that word tends to dominate the way you see yourself and your past. I think of a bright woman whose self-identity was fused with the word "dummy," a moniker her critical father had teased her with. Despite being college educated, she battled that feeling for decades. Perhaps the word is embedded in an early memory—more sensed than verbalized. In either case, pinpointing the word for your pain will

allow you to *express* it—like draining an infected wound—so you can move beyond it. Whatever your word is, write it down.

_____

5. Rate how distressing that word is on a scale from 0 to 10, with 0 being no distress and 10 being the most distress you can imagine feeling.

    Write it down. _____

6. Now, welcome that memory into full, accepting, kind awareness—not as an enemy you are fighting, but as a friend you are welcoming into your home. Not with the thought, "I'll grit my teeth and tolerate this for a minute so I can get rid of it," but rather, "I welcome this memory fully into kind awareness." Let your body be soft and relaxed. Think of that friend in your home, near a warm fireplace.

7. With this kind and open attitude, repeat aloud—loudly—the single word that you selected in step 4, as many times as you can in forty-five seconds. When finished, rate your distress level from 0 to 10.

    Write it down. _____

8. Notice what has happened. Do you notice that the word loses some of its emotional impact? That it is just a word? Do you feel less fused with the word? Is the memory or the word less distressing? Do you realize that you really *can* bear it? If so, this might be a good skill to use with other distressing experiences. It is powerful to invite our pain into open, kind awareness, and notice how the way we experience the memory shifts.

9. Now try repeating the word again for about forty-five seconds, this time varying how you repeat it. Say it loud, then soft. Slow, then fast. Falsetto, then low in pitch. Try it in a scolding tone, like nasty old Aunt Edna would use, then in a playful tone. Then try repeating the word with a kind tone. These variations can further help change the way you experience the memory. Again, rate your distress level from 0 to 10.

    Write it down. _____

I've seen this strategy profoundly change people's reaction to memories. One nurse became nauseated whenever she thought of a shaming memory. After trying this, her husband noticed that she could for the first time talk about the memory without negative reactions. If this technique was helpful, you might with caution try it with other memories that are more distressing, including earlier memories.

Other Applications for Defusion

You might employ the defusing strategy with other words that carry a painful charge. To identify such words, Follette and Pistorello (2007, 124) suggest considering the following:

- I secretly fear that I am _____, but most people around me would not know that about me.

- I get angriest when people imply or say that I am _____.

- To my parent figure, the worst quality for someone to have was/is _____.

If you don't remember the specific memory that triggers these words, simply bring the word into kind, open awareness, experiencing all the emotions and bodily sensations. Then repeat the word for forty-five seconds and notice what happens.

Carrying on with Pain

To further solidify the idea that you can let your pain into awareness and then leave the battlefield to carry on with your valued life, try this exercise. On a sheet of paper, draw a picture of a big head. Inside, place everything that is going on in your head—the feelings, sensations, thoughts, and images. Again, do this with a kind, accepting attitude and a soft, relaxed body. Then fold the paper up and put it in your pocket as you go about your day. This symbolizes the fact that you can bear your pain and carry on with your life. You can acknowledge the pain without letting it hold you back from the things you most want to do.

Defusing with Humor

If you wish to approach pain with a playful touch of humor, try this. Stand up. Put your weight mostly over one foot as you slouch and slump in a shamed posture. Let your head drop. Dolefully say aloud, "I'm inadequate." Really let the painful feeling of that statement sink in with an accepting attitude. Shift your weight to the other foot and say, "I'm inadequate." Now bend your knees, with your hands behind you, as though you were going to do a standing broad jump. Throw your fingers straight up in the air toward the ceiling and wiggle your fingers, as you jump up into the air and with a big smile say, "I'm inadequate." Do that two more times. You might chuckle at the incongruity of what is happening as you do this. When we chuckle, we heal. Notice how the experience of being inadequate changes. You've now used the principle of reconsolidation, weaving in humor and physical movement to change the way you experience inadequacy, which everyone feels at times. Of course, you can do this exercise with any other shaming label.

Track Your Results

Repeat the defusing technique three times, once a day over a three-day period, and fill out your Skills Record (see appendix A). You might then wish to give one or more of the other defusing applications a try, logging those in your Skills Record as well.

CHAPTER 22

How Would the World Be Different?

Do thoughts of shame continually trouble you? Thoughts like, "I'm inadequate, incompetent, no good"? Do they weigh you down or make you anxious? Do you fight or run from these thoughts, get uptight at the thoughts, or constantly try to fix yourself?

This strategy is a very useful way to transform this experience into a quiet, realistic sense of worth by asking you to reflect on two questions (Ulrich 1992):

1. How would the world be different—in a bad way—if everyone were like you?

2. How would the world be different—in a good way—if everyone were like you?

The first question encourages you to acknowledge weaker areas, while the second encourages you to clearly see your strengths. It's good—and curiously settling—to honestly and without judging acknowledge weaknesses. You face reality and realize the world doesn't end. It's even more important (and motivating) to recognize your strengths. For people raised in a shame-based environment, it is especially important to honestly identify strengths.

Soon you'll take your time to ponder these important questions. But first, here is an example of someone who thoughtfully completed this exercise.

1. How would the world be different—in a bad way—if everyone were like you? In this step describe the ways it would be worse.

   Everyone would be shy, reserved, holding back, introverted, lacking confidence, slow to react to emergencies, self-doubting (Am I good enough? I must try hard to impress others), anxious, serious, not playful, guilty, low in self-esteem, awkward in social settings, intimidated by authority figures, uncertain and untrusting in relationships.

2. How would the world be different—in a good way—if everyone were like you?

   People would be very respectful of others. Everyone would understand and be kind to those struggling and suffering. There would be more listening to each other. People would appreciate moments of amusement with each other. People would relate and empathize, not judge.

People would obey laws. No one would commit crimes or intentionally hurt others. People would earnestly try to do their best, learn from their mistakes, and improve for their own benefit and the benefit of others. People would share their life lessons with loved ones. They'd take joy in people's successes and accomplishments. Everyone would give a leg up to those in need. There would be no bragging or feelings of superiority. People would be deliberate and careful. They'd want others to succeed and be happy. They'd be fully present with others and show interest in their lives and well-being. There would be no wars.

Now it's your turn to reflect on these questions using the following worksheet. A copy of this worksheet is also available at http://www.newharbinger.com/46646.

How the World Would Be Different

Now try to reflect on these two questions in writing. Take all the time you need. Put them aside and return a day or two later to see what comes up. Be thorough. After you complete responding to the two questions, process what you have written.

1. How would the world be different—in a bad way—if everyone were like me? In this step describe the ways it would be worse.

_____

_____

_____

_____

_____

_____

_____

_____

_____

2. How would the world be different—in a good way—if everyone were like me?

_____

_____

_____

_____

_____

_____

_____

_____

_____

_____

_____

_____

_____

Processing Your Responses

In your journal, reflect upon what you have written:

1. Notice that everyone has weaknesses and everyone has strengths, without exception. That makes you, in one sense, just like everyone else.

2. Look at your list of weaknesses with full awareness, only acknowledge them with compassion, loving-kindness, and full clarity, rather than a vague sense of uneasiness. Look on them as you might look at a beloved child or best friend who hasn't yet learned how to overcome these

weaknesses and turn them into strengths. Notice how your body feels as you acknowledge your weaknesses in this way. Do you notice that this response to weakness is somewhat settling? Does your body feel calmer? More at ease? Take your time with this step.

3. Notice your strengths. How does it feel to do this? Perhaps this is a new experience to appreciate that some of your strengths are assets that make (or can make) the world better. Your mix of strengths and weaknesses is unique, making you different from anyone else.

4. Consider that your strengths—and also your weaknesses—reflect a starting point from which to grow. With patience and compassion, these areas can work together to help you flourish over time.

5. Does this exercise heighten your appreciation for people whose strengths complement your own, lift your spirits, and inspire you?

6. Does this exercise suggest that your strengths are, or can be, of value to yourself and others? Does it help you feel like you have a place in the world?

CHAPTER 23

Prepare for the Return of Shame

As you move ahead after gaining mastery of shame skills, it is not uncommon for shame to reappear at times. For example, unkind treatment might stir up old feelings of shame related to ACEs. It is extremely helpful to be prepared for such times by anticipating them and having preplanned responses at the ready. This activity was developed by trauma expert Marybeth Williams (Williams and Poijula 2013). Read through some constructive shame responses that others have come up with; then you'll have an opportunity to write down your own.

1. When I am with people who still try to shame me, I can…

    -   Smile and think, "No matter what you do or say, I know I am a worthwhile person."

    -   Use my self-compassion statements.

    -   Soothe my body with my favorite body-based skills.

    -   Calmly and with dignity walk away.

    -   Ignore the person, thinking that it is probably their own shame that causes them to act that way.

2. When I am feeling shamed, I can tell myself (and be willing to try to believe)…

    -   My worth as a person is infinite, unchanging, and equal to others'.

    -   Thoughts and feelings of shame are just that—thoughts and feelings that come and go. I am deeper than what I think and feel.

    -   No matter what, I choose to love myself—right now!

    -   Why should I worry about what another imperfect person thinks?

3. If shameful feelings return, or if someone tries to shame me, I can nurture myself by…

    -   Doing the five-minute head-to-toe stress reducer.

    -   Taking care of my physical health—take a warm shower, go for a pleasant walk, have a nutritious meal, and get sufficient sleep.

- Cheering myself on ("Way to go…you are trying").
- Smiling as I reach beneath the shame to experience my true, happy, worthwhile nature.

The following worksheet affords a wonderful opportunity to review the shame skills you have learned and organize a response that is best suited to you. You might even come up with new ideas for coping with shame that you hadn't previously considered. A copy of this worksheet is also available at http://www .newharbinger.com/46646.

Planned Responses to Shame

List three responses for each of the following questions:

1. When I am with people who still try to shame me, I can…

    _____

    _____

    _____

2. When I am feeling shamed, I can tell myself (and be willing to try to believe)…

    _____

    _____

    _____

3. If shameful feelings return, or if someone tries to shame me, I can nurture myself by…

    _____

    _____

    _____

Put aside your responses to the three questions for a day or two. Then return and make any adjustments you wish to make. When you are satisfied with your written plan, mentally rehearse. See yourself experiencing shame. Without judging, notice what that feels like in your body. Then see yourself using the coping responses that you have identified. Track to see what has changed with your body, emotions, thoughts, or images.

Track Your Results

Do this exercise daily for three consecutive days, and complete your Skills Record (see appendix A).

Moving Forward

CHAPTER 24

Cultivate Self-Respect

Thus far, this workbook has focused on healing emotional pain resulting from adverse childhood experiences—pain inflicted by others. In this chapter, you'll take a look at shame that you might have wittingly or unwittingly caused yourself—and how to begin to heal that shame and replace it with self-respect.

To have self-respect is to have a quiet, inner gladness to be you. Part of this gladness stems from the inner peace of knowing that you have good character—not that you are perfect, but that you are trying your best to elevate yourself and others. Character describes your basic nature. When you can feel that your basic nature is good, that you are trustworthy, and that you have a good reputation with yourself, then you'll tend to feel inner gladness—a sense of inner peace and self-respect that is key to self-esteem and well-being.

Hopefully, if you have worked your way to this point in the workbook, you have made significant progress in reworking shame caused by other people or events. Now, let's turn to taking responsibility for changing self-chosen patterns that trigger or add to old feelings of shame.

Understanding Self-Inflicted Shame

The renowned psychologist Abraham Maslow (1968, 5) lucidly wrote:

> The serious thing for each person to recognize vividly and poignantly, each for himself, is that every falling away from species-virtue, every crime against one's own nature, every evil act, *every one without exception records itself* in our unconscious and makes us despise ourselves. Karen Horney had a good word to describe this unconscious perceiving and remembering; she said it "registers." If we do something we are ashamed of, it "registers" to our discredit, and if we do something honest or fine or good, it "registers" to our credit. The net results ultimately are either one or the other—either we respect and accept ourselves or we despise ourselves and feel contemptible, worthless, and unlovable. Theologians used to use the word "*accidie*" to describe the sin of failing to do with one's life all that one knows one could do.

Maslow went on to say that real guilt is not being true to yourself, to your own intrinsic nature—betraying yourself. Such guilt is necessary to our development, an inner guide for reaching our potential. We'll distinguish here real, or reasonable, guilt, from chronic, exaggerated guilt and shame. Real guilt is helpful—it helps us change behaviors that cause us suffering. Then guilt is best released. Chronic, exaggerated guilt and shame serve no useful purpose.

Good Character

Good character makes us likable and trustworthy to ourselves and others. It also provides inner strength that protects us in distressing times. Conversely, an unfavorable opinion of our character is painful and distressing. Interestingly, researchers in the Netherlands studied eight assumptions held by health care professionals and people with post-traumatic complaints. The assumptions related to how people viewed themselves, the goodness of the world and other people, and events. They found that self-worth had the strongest association with post-traumatic symptoms compared with the other assumptions. Self-worth—"the individual's assumption that he or she is a good, moral, worthy, and decent individual" (van Bruggen et al. 2018, 816)—was measured by four items:

- I often think that I am no good at all.

- I have a low opinion of myself.

- I have reason to be ashamed of my personal character.

- I am very satisfied with the kind of person I am. (reverse score)

They concluded that this finding was in line with "the wide recognition [that] self-worth [is] an important factor in the development of psychopathology" (Zeigler-Hill 2011, cited in van Bruggen et al., 2018, 823).

Where and Why We Get into Trouble

Each of us has done things that have registered to our discredit. Perhaps we were young, inexperienced, careless, curious, or reacting to pain that we didn't know how to handle at the time. This is what imperfect mortals do as we strive to figure out what truly makes us happy and what makes life most satisfying. Although we can't change our history, we can learn from our experiences—changing our lives from a past of regrets to a record of "lessons finally learned" (Harrison 2012, A-19). Rather than view ourselves with harsh judgment and self-contempt, we can strive to take a look at how well our choices have worked for us, and then make needed course corrections.

The Two Keys to Self-Respect

There are two keys to building self-respect: 1) stop doing what hurts us or others, and 2) develop character strengths that promote inner peace. Both keys start with awareness and understanding of our habitual patterns, a grasp of healing principles, and an awareness of new coping possibilities.

Healing Principles

These principles will guide the two activities that follow:

• Past choices and behaviors are not a reflection of your higher nature and potential. Although they may be imprinted on your nervous system, they are simply past choices and behaviors. They do not define your true nature.

• The goal is to use past experience to motivate movement to a higher way of being—one that is true to your higher nature. Without self-condemnation or shame, we simply notice where we've been and where we'd like to go. At the same time, we acknowledge the good we have done. This counters the erroneous notion that we are all bad and motivates us to build upon past successes.

• The standard is not perfection. If it were, no one would have inner peace. Rather, we are striving to reach our ideal character, with a hefty dose of kindness for the times we fall short. And when we stumble and fall, we dust ourselves off and keep going, knowing that character is developed through persistence over a lifetime.

• Ultimately, we will be able to feel satisfaction as we look back over our lives and think, "I made mistakes, to be sure, but I know I've tried my best to learn from my mistakes and live a good life."

Stopping Harmful Behaviors

To stop self-destructive behavior, it is not enough to simply stop doing the behavior. You must find a replacement behavior that better meets your underlying needs. Think about the ways you have coped with stress in the past—ways that have not worked well, or perhaps have gotten you into trouble. In a moment, you'll be asked to fill out a worksheet to gain insights as to what unfulfilled needs might be driving your unsuccessful old ways of coping, gauge how effective these old ways have been, and identify new ways of coping that might replace the shame-inducing coping methods. Here is an example of how one individual completed this worksheet.

Old Ways of Coping	Need I Was Trying to Fill	How Well This Has Worked	New Ways of Coping
Anger. I blow up at others who find fault with me.	Protect myself against painful shame.	Seems to push people away. Makes me disappointed in myself.	Understand and accept people's imperfections. Forgive. Be patient. Befriend. Accept myself.
Denial. I can't admit when I'm wrong.	Protect myself from shame and pain.	I'm spared some pain of being wrong, but I can't improve what I deny. People argue with me, then give up.	Acknowledge weaknesses with kind acceptance and a smile.
I escape my inner pain with addictions (work, drugs, shopping).	Avoid pain.	Temporary relief; the pain didn't change. The addiction created more problems.	Acknowledge and soothe my pain with compassion.
I seek comfort and happiness in addictions.	Happiness.	I gained some pleasure, but not the deep happiness I desire.	Find happiness within—use spiritual resources.
I'm critical of myself.	Fix myself; protect myself from the shame of the same old mistakes.	Harsh criticism is deflating and depressing.	Motivate myself with encouragement.
Isolation	Protects me from the pain of rejection.	It makes me feel lonely.	Discern people's character, and open my heart to letting trustworthy people in, little by little.

Love tends to neutralize fear, allowing us to see calmly and with deeper understanding where we are and where we'd like to be. So complete the following worksheet with a spirit of great compassion and insight. A copy of this worksheet is also available at http://www.newharbinger.com/46646.

New Ways of Coping

1. In the first column, describe how you have typically reacted in the past to stress.

2. In the second column, identify the needs that you were trying to fill with this way of coping.

3. In the third column, describe how well this way of coping worked. You might find that there were some gains. If there were none, you probably would have abandoned the behavior by now.

4. In the fourth column, describe new ways of coping that might better meet your needs. If you don't have a better option, you will likely fall back into the old ways of coping. Don't worry at this point if the new coping options seem out of reach. This activity is simply to assess where you are and to identify new possibilities that *might* work better for you. It can be quite empowering simply to be aware of new coping options that you perhaps hadn't seriously considered before.

Cultivate Self-Respect   159

Old Ways of Coping	Need I Was Trying to Fill	How Well This Has Worked	New Ways of Coping

Building Character

There is general consensus around the world regarding the character strengths that are most prized. These character strengths promote community and team building. They foster trust and respect in others. Perhaps most importantly, they promote self-respect and inner peace. The following exercise will help you see where you are with regard to these character strengths, recognize that you already possess them at some level of development, and set a course to develop them more fully. Again, love tends to neutralize fear, allowing us to see more clearly. So complete this inventory with kindness and curiosity.

Integrity Meditation

"Integrity" means living in harmony with our deepest values. Integrity brings a sense of well-being—self-respect, inner peace, happiness, and trust. Sitting quietly, consider this question: Is there anything that disturbs your peace, damages your reputation with yourself, or leads you or others to distrust you? Just calmly and curiously notice what comes up, without judging or criticizing yourself. Notice where in your body you experience what is coming up. Breathe into that area.

The next step in building character is to take a kind moral inventory. The following exercise is adapted from Schiraldi (2017). A copy of this worksheet is also available at http://www.newharbinger.com/46646.

Fearless, Searching, Loving Moral Inventory

Read the definitions of the character strengths. Make any adjustments to these definitions that you feel are appropriate. In the second column, rate where you presently stand. The third column helps to motivate improvement by reminding you of strengths and potentialities that already exist. The fourth column asks you to identify specific steps that will bring you closer to character excellence.

For example, to increase honesty you might keep an Honesty–Dishonesty journal for a week. Each day, list:

Lies you hear. How does it feel to hear them?

Lies (even "white lies") that you tell. How does it feel to tell them? Does it make you happier?

Truths you tell (especially give yourself credit for telling the truth when truth-telling is difficult). How does that make you feel inside?

At the end of the week, see how you did. Then set a goal for improvement. For example, you might aim to go an entire day (or some other reachable goal) only telling the truth—no white lies, deceit, or excuses to save face. Ask yourself, "What is the worst that could happen if I told the truth? What is the best thing that could happen?"

Character Strength	Rate yourself from 1 to 10, where 10 means you are living this strength as well as a person can.	Describe a time in the past when you demonstrated this strength.	Describe what you could do to demonstrate this strength better and more often.
Courage means persisting in doing the right thing despite the pressure to do otherwise.			
Honesty means you speak only the truth, always. No "white lies," half-truths (truth can be tactful and kind), cheating, or stealing.			
Integrity means your behaviors match your values and that you show your sincere, authentic self without pretense.			
Respect means you honor people and treat them as worthwhile, and you are civil and courteous.			

Character Strength	Rate yourself from 1 to 10, where 10 means you are living this strength as well as a person can.	Describe a time in the past when you demonstrated this strength.	Describe what you could do to demonstrate this strength better and more often.
Fairness means you play by the rules, do not take dishonorable advantage of others, and treat others impartially.			
Loyalty, faithfulness, and **trustworthiness** mean you keep commitments and confidences, don't speak ill of others behind their backs, and are reliable.			
Responsibility means being able and willing to respond to valid needs and duties, being dependable, and protecting yourself and others.			
Kindness and **caring** mean you are concerned for the welfare of others, and desire to help and support their growth; you are considerate, generous, and tenderhearted.			

Character Strength	Rate yourself from 1 to 10, where 10 means you are living this strength as well as a person can.	Describe a time in the past when you demonstrated this strength.	Describe what you could do to demonstrate this strength better and more often.
Sexual integrity means your sexual expression is used in the context of love and concern for the other, and never used in a selfish or exploitive way.			
Tolerance means you are patient and forgiving with the differences and imperfections of others.			
Humility means you see everyone as worthwhile as you are, you can learn from everyone, and you have faults and much to learn, just like everyone else.			
Gratitude means you feel appreciation and awe for all of life's loveliness— things great and small.			

The following exercise asks you to explore character strengths more deeply. A copy of this worksheet is also available at http://www.newharbinger.com/46646.

Grow Character Strengths

1. First, pick a character strength you'd like to grow. Then complete this sentence stem, writing as many responses as you can think of (this can be very motivating):

    The positive consequences of my being more _____ (honest, kind, tolerant, etc.) are...

    _____

    _____

    _____

    _____

2. Next, carry out actions to grow this character strength. For at least the next three days, practice the actions you identified in the fourth column of the "Fearless, Searching, Loving Moral Inventory" previously. Write the actions here:

    _____

    _____

    _____

    _____

    _____

    _____

    _____

    _____

Be patient. Persist. Character doesn't grow overnight. Expect setbacks. Keep trying. The fruits of your efforts might grow gradually, but they will grow.

Reflections on Character Strength

The following quotations may help you reflect on character strengths.

- "Character…is crucial to a person's identity and sense of self-worth." (Hara Estroff Marano)

- "Be at peace with your own soul, then heaven and earth will be at peace with you." (Saint Isaac of Nineveh)

- "No person can be truly at peace with himself if he does not live up to his moral capacity." (Norman Cousins)

- [What's it like being a living saint?] "You have to be holy in your position as you are, and I have to be holy in the position that God has put me… Holiness is a simple duty for you and for me. So it is nothing extraordinary to be holy." (Mother Teresa)

- "Set your heart on doing good. Do it over and over again, and you will be filled with joy. A fool is happy until his mischief turns against him. And a good man may suffer until his goodness flowers." (Buddha)

- "Live a good, honorable life. Then when you get older, and think back, you'll be able to enjoy it a second time." (Dalai Lama)

Track Your Results

Record your experience with growing a character strength in your Skills Record (see appendix A). If you had a positive experience, you might wish to continue to grow the other character strengths.

CHAPTER 25

Forgive Old Wounds

The world is full of light—resilient people who inspire us. Perhaps you remember the photograph taken in 1972 and seen around the world of Kim Phuc Phan Thi. Kim Phuc is the nine-year-old Vietnamese girl seen running down a dirt road, screaming in agony from napalm burns that seared her little body to the bone. In a flash, her life changed from idyllic happiness to unrelenting pain. In a culture that prized beauty, her scars dashed her dreams of marrying. Former friends shunned her. At least she thought she could become a doctor to help similarly scarred children, but the North Vietnamese government pulled her out of school to use her as a propaganda pawn. Becoming so depressed, she planned suicide as a release from her pain.

Kim Phuc eventually hit upon the idea of forgiving her enemies and wishing them well. She realized that she had harbored bitterness toward so many people: the pilot who accidentally burned her, the communists who crushed her dreams, those who had shunned and disowned her, those who destroyed her home, and even everyday people who couldn't relate to her pain. Though difficult, she began praying for those who had mistreated her and wishing them well. Gradually, almost imperceptibly, she found that her heart was softening. Her natural, infectious smile and inner peace returned. She was even invited to become a spokesperson for the United Nations, speaking around the world about replacing hatred with peace and love. The photo that she once could not bear to look at now reminds her with gratitude of those she has been able to help. In her inspiring book, titled *Fire Road* (Phan Thi 2017), Kim Phuc writes that we all have our fire roads, and we must discover a path to replacing bitterness with love.

Once considered only a theological concept, forgiveness is now firmly established in the psychological research as a means to restore inner peace and self-esteem in survivors of toxic stress (Enright 2012). As we have discussed, we cannot change our histories, but we can change our response to our histories. Forgiveness affords us the opportunity to respond in a way that reconnects us with our innate wise and loving nature.

Principles of Forgiveness

A clear understanding of the nature of forgiveness will help you in your journey to forgive wounds caused by ACEs and other offenses. So let's clarify the principles of forgiveness.

- Forgiveness does not gloss over the serious harm that the offender caused. To do so is a form of denial that actually blocks healing. Rather, we forgive after we fully acknowledge the pain so that we can heal that pain. (Recall the principle of reconsolidation, page 46.) Then we choose to release anger, hatred, and the desire to hurt the offender so that we are no longer poisoned by bitterness.

- Forgiving serious offenses is neither simple nor easy! Yet this difficult process yields enormous dividends.

- Some claim that forgiving is helpful but not necessary. I say it is necessary, but it should be done prudently, and only when the time is right.

- Forgiveness is a personal choice we make to replace anger with love. This choice is made independent of the severity of the offense—and irrespective of whether or not the offender deserves forgiveness, apologizes, or asks for forgiveness. The choice to forgive is totally dependent on our willingness to change our response to the past. We choose to forgive because we have seen that others who have chosen to do so have been liberated from consuming bitterness.

- Whether the offender is a caregiver, someone else, or yourself, forgiveness extends compassion to the wrongdoer, knowing that those who willfully hurt others do so from a dark place, an inner sickness that is inconsistent with inner peace and happiness.

- The highest form of forgiveness not only releases anger and a desire for revenge but also wishes the offender well.

- Forgiveness does not necessarily mean reconciling with an untrustworthy offender. (Reconciliation *might* come once trust has been restored.) Neither does forgiveness necessarily mean forgetting. Indeed, you may choose to seek justice for an offender when that could serve to protect yourself or others. However, seeking justice is best done with a sense of purpose, not a spirit of vengeance.

There are four phases to the forgiveness process: feeling forgiveness, forgiving yourself, forgiving others, and seeking forgiveness. We'll explore these, and their related skills, in turn.

Feel Forgiveness

Every one of us makes mistakes. Without exception, every one of us has gotten turned around at times. How fortunate is the person who has experienced genuine forgiveness! Have you ever felt this? Has anyone ever communicated to you that they forgive you for the mistakes you have made and still love you? If so, reflect for a moment on how that felt. Sometimes, people who think of a loving and forgiving deity can draw upon this experience. I was once explaining this principle to a group of veterans. Afterward, an old salty and somewhat scary Navy veteran approached me and said, "I don't believe in a supreme being, but I am troubled by regrets from what I did years ago. What can I do?" I shared with him this strategy (Litz et al. 2016).

Instructions

Think of a time when you did something wrong or failed to do something right, and this has deeply troubled you. Now imagine being in the presence of a kind, loving moral authority who has your back, wants you to be happy, and does not want you to suffer anymore. This kind moral authority might be God or a higher power, a spiritual guide, a trusted friend or relative, or an imagined figure. In quiet reflection, imagine feeling surrounded by this figure's compassion as you share your pain—what you have done or failed to do, and how this has affected you. Imagine that kind moral authority holding your pain with deep caring and full presence. Notice the pain releasing as you breathe out. On the in-breath, imagine breathing in the compassion that emanates from this kind presence. On the out-breath feel that compassion bathe and wash over all parts of your body. Notice how that feels in your body. Listen to what that presence kindly shares.

Perhaps the kind moral authority explains that you were younger, inexperienced, or in pain then. Perhaps your emotions got the best of you. You hadn't fully learned a better way of coping. Perhaps fear or self-doubt got in your way, or you made a decision under duress. Perhaps you deserve partial credit for the good you did. Perhaps you hear confidence expressed that you will learn and improve from that difficult time—that your experience has taught you wisdom that will help you and others in the future. Perhaps you are reassured that your mistakes do not define you, that you are more than your mistakes. The kind moral authority reminds you that it's okay to feel the pain and guilt, learn from it, and then release it. If shame was imprinted in your earlier years, perhaps you are reminded that the forgiving process might be more difficult and might require extra time, compassion, and patience. You might imagine this loving figure embracing you or putting a reassuring hand on your shoulder.

Take a few breaths and track your body and emotions as you reflect upon this encounter. See yourself moving forward with inner peace and hope.

Forgive Yourself

Kaufman (1996, 254) has written, "For every wrong there is a punishment and also a statute of limitations." Ask yourself, "Have I suffered enough, too little, or too much?" You might also ask, "Is there something that would help me make amends—some meaningful way to repair any damage I've done?" Think about this for a few moments. We'll return to this shortly. Then try this reflection (Salzberg 1995).

Instructions

Get in a comfortable meditator's posture in a quiet place. Calm yourself in your breathing, and say aloud or to yourself: "For all the ways I have hurt or harmed myself or others wittingly or unwittingly, I offer forgiveness." Let this intention settle and track how this feels in your body. For every wrong that surfaces, repeat kindly, "I forgive myself," and track your sensations and emotions.

Some find it helpful to journal about past wrongs, writing down what they did or failed to do, what they thought and felt about that, and how that has impacted their lives. Write for fifteen to thirty minutes each day for three or four days. End with the written intention, "I now choose to release my guilt and forgive myself so that I can lead a more productive life."

Remember that this exercise is intended to help you identify a hurt, feel appropriate guilt and sadness, learn and grow from the experience, and then move beyond the guilt. This is done with the compassion of a kind parent or a best friend—not shame, which serves no constructive purpose.

Forgive Parents or Caregivers

Dominic was having trouble at work, getting into arguments with his boss and coworkers. At home he was angry and critical of his partner and children. Things got so bad that he sought therapy for his anger. Dominic had grown up with a very critical, emotionally abusive father. Learning about forgiveness, he approached his father and said, "I want you to know I forgive you for how you treated me." His father's eyes filled with tears and he gave his son a stiff, awkward embrace. The relationship didn't change, but Dominic changed. No longer angry, he improved his relationships at work and at home.

Alcoholics Anonymous members write that people in recovery come to realize that those who "wronged us were perhaps spiritually sick…We asked God to help us show them the same tolerance, pity, and patience that we would cheerfully grant a sick friend. When a person offended us, we said to ourselves, 'This is a sick man. How can I be helpful to him? God save me from being angry. Thy will be done'" (Anonymous Press 1992, 67).

Instructions

1. Prepare to meditate or write. Find a quiet, comfortable place.

2. Sit and calm yourself. Think briefly about the pain and wounding caused by an offending parent or caregiver. The core wound was feeling unloved and of no worth. Also, consider the sadness, fear, shame, or anger you felt. See your parent or caregiver sitting at a distance. Notice the pain shown in his or her face, body, speech, or gestures. How does that person carry pain? Where did

that pain come from? Image that adult as a once innocent child who was hurting. See that person surrounded with light and love. Consider that adult now:

- Why would he (or she) act that way? What's bothering him? How has life hurt her? Think how sad it is that she has shut down her heart. What might have blocked his happiness?

- Go back to his childhood. If you don't know it, imagine what would have made him that way.

- Consider that her hurting you was not personal—a reflection of her pain, not your worth.

- Imagine asking, "Why did you treat me that way?" See what comes up. Was that person happy? Or hurting and bitter?

3. Consider: Did any good result from your difficult experience? Did it make you stronger or wiser in any way? (For example, did it cause you to resolve to treat people more kindly, to try to understand the pain they are coming from? Did you realize you were strong to survive? Did you learn from your parent's good traits *and* bad? Did you give yourself a pat on the back for ways you've done better than your parent or caregiver?)

4. As best you can, say to yourself silently or aloud, "For whatever you did to hurt me, wittingly or unwittingly, I forgive you."

5. For each offense that surfaces, repeat with a soft heart, "I forgive you."

6. Relax your body. Breathe out, releasing, relaxing. Continue to track your breathing and your body.

Seek Forgiveness from Others

Often, addictions are driven by unresolved pain. People in recovery frequently come to see that their reactions to pain hurt others and require forgiveness from those they've hurt. In one addiction recovery meeting, we discussed how asking for forgiveness from those we've hurt often helps both the offender and the offended. AnnaMarie was puzzled by this, asking, "Why should I ask forgiveness of my parents, when they are the ones who hurt me?" Good point. It certainly is ideal if those who hurt us ask for forgiveness. How much easier it is to forgive those who sincerely acknowledge their wrongs and request forgiveness. However, those who hurt us were not whole at the time or they wouldn't have behaved so poorly. They might not be whole enough to ask your forgiveness now. Why, then, would you ask forgiveness of those who hurt you?

Seeking forgiveness from others accomplishes two things. First, it cleans up your side of the street. Without making excuses, you take responsibility for your imperfect behavior and try as best you can to repair the damage you've caused. (Sometimes a sincere apology and a commitment to try to improve are all you can do. Or you might commit to live the best life possible, serve others, take up a worthwhile cause, or contribute financially to a good cause.) Second, in seeking forgiveness, you sometimes soften the hearts of others, enabling them to move beyond grievances they might have with you.

Trying to make amends for what you have done and helping others heal is an important step in your healing. Sometimes two hearts heal when forgiveness is sought. When AnnaMarie was able to seek forgiveness from her parents for being so angry and rebellious, they softened, apologized, and expressed sorrow for being such imperfect parents. However, be cautioned that some people might not accept your apology or know how to respond constructively.

Instructions

1. Think about ways you have hurt other people. Do this without making excuses. If it is safe, plan a meeting with the offended person. Humbly acknowledge what you did or failed to do. You might simply tell the other person something like, "I hurt you. I was wrong. I'm sorry." Say this without justifying your actions or attacking the other person. Speak from the heart and accept the outcome.

2. If someone is unsafe or unavailable, you might consider writing your apology in a letter that you may or may not choose to mail.

Combined Forgiveness Meditation

Some people find that repeating in the same sitting the four intentions created or suggested by master healer Sharon Salzberg (1995, 95–96) is very healing. As with other scripts in the workbook, you can read and apply these instructions one at a time, have someone read them to you, or record and then listen to them.

Instructions

Sit comfortably, close your eyes if that is comfortable, and breathe abdominally. Let your mind settle. Allow time to reflect, without rushing, as you repeat, silently or aloud (whichever you prefer), the following four intentions. Pause with each intention, and then see what comes up. As different events, people, or images come up, simply repeat, as appropriate, "May I feel forgiveness," "I offer forgiveness," "I forgive you," or "I ask your forgiveness."

1. For all I did or failed to do, knowingly or unknowingly, that has harmed others or myself, may I feel forgiveness. (For each wrong that comes up, repeat, "May I feel forgiveness.")

2. For all of the ways I have hurt or harmed myself or others, knowingly or unknowingly, I offer myself forgiveness. (For each wrong, repeat, "I offer forgiveness.")

3. If anyone has hurt or harmed me, knowingly or unknowingly, I forgive them. (For each wrong, repeat, "I forgive you.")

4. If I have hurt or harmed anyone, knowingly or unknowingly, I ask their forgiveness. (For each wrong, repeat, "I ask your forgiveness.")

Track Your Results

Practice each of the exercises related to the four phases of forgiveness: feeling forgiven, forgiving yourself, forgiving others, and seeking forgiveness. Practice the skill related to each phase for three consecutive days before moving on to the next phase. Then practice the combined forgiveness meditation daily for three days. Record your experience with each of the activities in your Skills Record (see appendix A).

The seventeenth-century French writer François de La Rochefoucauld penned the words: "We forgive to the extent that we love." We forgive because we love ourselves and others, and because we wish ourselves and others peace. Consistent with the research, you might find that forgiving results in greater self-esteem and happiness, better mental health, less emotional distress, and fewer and less severe PTSD symptoms (for example, Cerci and Colucci 2017; Weinberg 2013; Worthington et al. 2007). However, forgiving serious offenses is difficult. Take your time. It is a process, not usually accomplished quickly or all at once. Practice forgiving patiently, repeatedly, and with great compassion.

CHAPTER 26

Feed the Soul

Ralph Waldo Emerson (1901) declared, "The one thing in the world, of value, is the active soul...this every [person] contains within...although, in almost all...obstructed, and as yet unborn." Close your eyes and see what comes up when you think of your soul. Pause to reflect; then write down what you get.

_____

_____

_____

_____

_____

To many people, the soul is the deepest part of us—the essence of our being, the core of who we are. You might have mentioned things like:

- The soul experiences the deepest, heartfelt emotions—peace, love, joy, hope—in response to beauty and goodness. The soul stands in awe of nature's grandeur and is moved to tears of tenderness when witnessing or receiving acts of kindness. The soul melts when witnessing the sweet innocence of a child.

- The soul is inspired by acts of courage or decency.

- The soul is intuitive, often drawing us to people, places, actions, or conclusions more by feelings than by logic.

- The soul is the seat of our worth, which is deeper than our imperfect behaviors, our imperfect bodies, or unkind treatment by others.

- The soul senses our infinite potential and capacities, and impels us to reach upward, beyond our present limitations.

- The soul is resilient, triumphing inwardly even when life's adversities cannot be changed.

- The soul possesses conscience, which distinguishes good from evil and impels us to be better.

- The soul is the purest part of us, where we feel the most at home. Like a flower, the enlightened soul seeks light and shrinks from evil, which diminishes our happiness and estranges us from ourselves, others, and divinity.

- The soul senses that there is more to us than the material world, and that there is something enduring and sturdy within.

- The soul yearns to love and be loved. The soul longs for deep connection to something bigger and better than ourselves, the divine. The soul also yearns for connection to our highest self and delights in connecting to the deepest good in others.

- The soul dreams and creates.

- The soul grows in wisdom from our life experience if our hearts are open to love.

In *The Untethered Soul*, Michael Singer (2007) reminds us that the soul is deeper and separate from what is happening to us. The soul is awareness that watches, but it is separate from our thoughts, emotions, or body. Thus, "I'm not good enough" is just a thought, just something that is sensed and experienced. Despite the sting of life's experiences, the core remains intact and capable of healing and growing.

We are in an interesting period in Western history. Spirituality is high, while religious participation is declining. Yet research has established upsides for both spirituality and religious practice. Let's try to define these terms.

Spirituality is the search for meaning and the sacred. Spirituality usually connotes connecting to something larger, something that transcends the self and the material universe. Psychiatrist George Vaillant (2008), who directed the longitudinal Harvard Study of Adult Development (The Grant Study), notes that spirituality is about the "language of the heart" (xi), an "amalgam of the positive emotions that bind us to other human beings—and to our experience of 'God'…Love, hope, joy, forgiveness, compassion, faith, awe, and gratitude are the spiritually important positive emotions" (4–5)…with love being "the shortest definition of spirituality" (16). Love and spirituality, he says, both result in "respect, appreciation, acceptance, sympathy, empathy, compassion, involvement, tenderness…gratitude" (16), connection, awe, and recognition of beauty. Finally, he notes that "reliance on a power greater than ourselves [is] found to be universal in cultures around the world" (20).

Religion refers to the practices and beliefs that aim to foster greater spirituality. In the scientific research, religiousness is usually measured by involvement or practice (for example, attending worship services, praying, reading sacred writings, striving to live ethically and charitably) and by having beliefs that provide solace during adversity (for example, believing that God is in control, is forgiving, and is glad to help us in our trials).

What the Research Says

Psychiatrist Harold Koenig has been at the forefront of spiritual and religious research. He reports that the majority of hundreds of studies find positive relationships between religion/spirituality and well-being (Koenig, King, and Carson 2012).

Studies have found that people who are religious or spiritual are, on average, happier, more resilient, mentally and physically healthier, and more forgiving of self and others. They also report higher self-esteem. For example, a study of nearly 2,000 Australian adolescents found that, compared to atheists and agnostics, those who believed in God had higher self-esteem and well-being (Huuskes et al. 2016). A large prospective Harvard study found that religiously involved teens—who prayed or meditated daily or attended weekly religious services—had better emotional well-being and resilience than those who were not religiously involved (Chen and VanderWeele 2018).

Among adults, those scoring high in spiritual health, including having a relationship with God, showed better outcomes on measures of self-esteem, hopelessness, and substance use (Hammermeister and Peterson 2001). In another study, religious coping (benevolent religious reappraisals, collaborative religious coping, and seeking spiritual support) was associated with higher self-esteem, while seeing God as punishing was associated with poorer psychological adjustment and more depression, anxiety, and stress (Ano and Vasconcelles 2005).

In veterans undergoing treatment for severe post-traumatic stress disorder, those who scored higher on adaptive dimensions of spirituality prior to starting treatment responded better to treatment than those who were low in adaptive spirituality (Currier, Holland, and Drescher 2015). Adaptive spirituality was defined as:

- Having a private spiritual practice, such as regular prayer and meditation

- Being involved in a church or other formal religious group

- Having daily spiritual experiences, such as feeling God's presence or love, finding comfort in religion or spirituality, feeling thankful for blessings

- Forgiving self and others and feeling forgiveness from God (or a higher power)

- Using positive religious coping—looking to God for strength and collaborating with God to solve problems

Statistics reveal patterns, but not necessarily the reasons for these patterns. So it is interesting to speculate as to the underlying reasons. McKenzie and Wright (1996) observed that God is the safest love object. Themes found in most world religions, such as the infinite worth of souls, infinite and healing divine love, compassion, and forgiveness, can assuage attachment disruptions and comfort the troubled soul. Koenig (1997) noted that while religion itself can provoke guilt, religion also provides a pathway to erasing guilt and making a fresh start. And most religious and spiritual orientations encourage taking personal responsibility for our behaviors, which tends to promote inner peace.

This is not to say that people who are spiritual or religious do not suffer. It is only to suggest that they tend to have certain resources that help get them through adversity. In reviewing the many studies on religion and spirituality, Koenig (2012) concluded that on balance, religion and spirituality are not a panacea, but generally are associated with greater well-being, improved coping with stress, and better mental health, including greater self-esteem, happiness, optimism, meaning and purpose, altruism, and marital stability, and less depression, anxiety, suicide, and drug and alcohol abuse.

There are some caveats suggested by the research. Religion seems to negatively affect emotional well-being only when:

- We have an unhappy image of deity, who might be viewed as punitive, unloving, or unrespon-sive. Thus, we might conclude that we do not matter and fail to draw upon spiritual resources. Note that attachment disruptions with parents can negatively color our view of deity. Understanding this can help us be patient and compassionate as we seek to cultivate spirituality.

- We are spiritually ambivalent. Holding, but not living, our beliefs can undermine inner peace and spiritual security. Spiritual uncertainty can also be unsettling. For example, agnostics are less happy than atheists, who are less happy than believers (Brooks 2008).

Nourishing the Soul: Spiritual Healing Imagery

To many people, nourishing the soul is as important as feeding the body. Alcoholics Anonymous notes that we must find a spiritual basis for life, or else we will seek peace and comfort in addictions (or distrac-tions). That peace and comfort is transient, not the abiding happiness we seek. The remainder of this chapter will suggest ways to nourish your soul, starting with this spiritual healing imagery. As with other scripts in the workbook, you can read and apply these instructions one at a time, have someone read them to you, or record and then listen to them.

Instructions

1. Sit comfortably in the meditator's posture. Relax into your breathing.

2. Notice if you experience any lingering emotional discomfort…(Pause.) If so, where in your body do you experience this discomfort?…(Pause.)

3. Give that discomfort a size, a shape, and a color. In other words, notice the boundaries of the discomfort, and then the color of that discomfort.

4. Now push the discomfort away from your body. See that discomfort forming a barrier in front of you. Notice the barrier's size, shape, color, and boundaries.

5. Now imagine walking around that barrier. And when you get to the other side, you see a loving figure: a kind, warm, and welcoming presence. That figure might be God, a higher power, or a real or imagined spiritual figure.

6. See yourself walking slowly toward that kind, loving figure. As you do, you feel the love and compassion emanating from that kind figure and penetrating your body. You open your arms and embrace that figure, and feel yourself embraced by that loving figure. And in that embrace your heart feels at peace…at home…safe.

7. Sit quietly for a few moments with those feelings.

Reflections on the Soul

The following quotations may help you reflect on the nature of the soul.

- "With all your science, can you tell me how it is that light comes into the soul?" (Henry David Thoreau)

- "Science and technology cannot replace the age-old spiritual values that have been largely responsible for the true progress of world civilization as we know it today." (Dalai Lama)

- "Science without religion is lame; religion without science is blind." (Albert Einstein)

- "All souls are capable of loving." (Saint Teresa of Ávila)

- "The splendor of the rose and the whiteness of the lily do not rob the little violet of its scent, nor the daisy of its simple charm…The world of our souls is like a garden in the eyes of God." (Saint Thérèse of Lisieux)

- "The will of God will never lead you where the grace of God cannot keep you." (Michael Catt)

- "To be able to bring His peace, joy, and love, we must have it ourselves, for we cannot give what we have not got. This requires that we spend time with God, look at Him, open our hearts to Him, and empty our hearts of all that is not Him." (Mother Teresa)

- "God speaks in the silence of our hearts, and we listen." (Mother Teresa)

- "Our creator is the same and never changes despite the names given Him by people here and in all parts of the world. Even if we gave Him no name at all, He would still be there within us, waiting to give us good on this earth." (George Washington Carver)

- "Life in Ravensbrück [concentration camp] took place on two separate levels, mutually impossible. One, the observable, external life, grew every day more horrible. The other, the life we lived with God, grew daily better, truth upon truth, glory upon glory." (Corrie ten Boom)

- "All I have seen teaches me to trust the creator for all I have not seen." (Ralph Waldo Emerson)

- "The deepest consolation comes from one's relationship to the divine." (Arthur Ashe)

- "Peace is not freedom from conflict or troubles but rather a calm assurance of our good standing before God." (D. Kelly Ogden)

Some people reflect best through writing out their ideas and feelings. The following worksheet is meant to help you reflect on sources of spirituality that could uplift you in distressing times. A copy of this worksheet is also available at http://www.newharbinger.com/46646.

Reflect Through Writing

Ponder the questions below. Then write down the thoughts that come to mind.

1. Where do you find solace, meaning, or uplift?

_____

_____

_____

_____

_____

2. Are there spiritual or religious practices that might nourish your soul? Some people consider meditation, reading sacred writings, prayer, joining a faith community, spending time in nature, worshipping, participating in healing rituals, taking time to feel God's presence, and so forth.

_____

_____

_____

_____

_____

3. Michael Singer (2007, 46) has stated, "The greatest gift one can give to God is to be pleased with His creation." As God's creation—or a fellow traveler and equally worthwhile human being with all others—how might you experience more joy in being you?

_____

_____

_____

_____

4. Often our spirituality is colored by the way our parents interacted with us. Are there any assumptions influenced by your parents or caregivers that might be interfering with gaining comfort from your spiritual/religious beliefs? For example, you might think: "God is mean, just like my parents. Nobody really cares about me. My mistakes are not to be forgiven or forgotten. I must be perfect." What might happen if you challenged such assumptions?

_____

_____

_____

_____

Adversity often opens people up to greater spiritually. Sometimes, however, toxic stress can numb people's feelings, including spiritual sensitivities. If childhood adversity has shut down your feelings, take heart. You _can_ heal emotionally. Once you are on the road to healing, you might notice your heart opening to tender spiritual experiences. Like many other skills in this workbook, though, the quest for greater spirituality is usually a gradual process. Give the process time, patience, and compassion as you discover what best nourishes your soul.

CHAPTER 27

Weave Joy into Your Life

One of the critical tasks of life is to learn how to enjoy it, despite life's inevitable adversities.

Recall that the skilled attachment figure teaches the child not only to be calm, but also to have joy—to play and have fun with life. If you didn't have a caregiver who helped you learn how to enjoy life by smiling, laughing, and playing with you, and by finding joy in life's simple pleasures, here is an opportunity to re-parent yourself—to celebrate life with all its wholesome pleasures.

Weaving joy into our lives helps us counterbalance adversities—reducing cortisol (Speer and Delgado 2017), lifting mood, and helping us be more resistant to depression (Askelund et al. 2019). In people recovering from substance use problems, taking just four minutes daily to practice happiness exercises helped them succeed in recovery (Hoeppner et al. 2019). (Joy and happiness are closely related. Think of happiness as experiencing positive emotions, such as joy and contentment, on a fairly regular basis, plus the sense that you and your life are worthwhile. Across cultures, self-esteem and happiness are closely linked.)

You might think of yourself, with a hint of survivor's pride, as being in recovery from childhood adversity. Having learned healing skills, you'll turn now to mastering some joy and happiness skills that perhaps you didn't master when you were preoccupied with surviving ACEs.

It is never too late to "create a joyful childhood," which is another way of saying getting better and better at healing and living joyfully. Like any other skill, joy skills take practice. The benefits accrue over time. This chapter will invite you to take time to be joyful. We'll explore seven simple joy skills. To start, practice each one once.

Remember the Good Times

1. Following are joyful *cue words* or phrases that call up pleasant memories: *Delight, peace, contentment, calm, love, gratitude, joy, tenderness, amusement, curiosity, confidence, wonder, belief in your own intrinsic goodness, healthy pride for something you've done.*

2. Pick a cue word or phrase, and recall in detail a specific memory related to it for sixty seconds. Think of a specific time and place and a memory that lasted no longer than a day (Askelund et al. 2019).

3. Track what it feels like in your body to recall this pleasant moment. Track your emotions.

4. Repeat this exercise for two or three more cue words or phrases.

Relive Happy Moments

Collect one or more photos capturing happy moments in your life—or look at one or two on your phone. For each, enter text describing what was happening in the picture. When you are finished writing, savor the moment for a minute or two (Hoeppner et al. 2019).

Savor with Gratitude

At the end of the day, describe in writing two positive experiences you noticed and appreciated from that day. Briefly describe what happened, what you thought, and what you felt—both your emotions and the sensations in your body. What about that experience was special to you?

Explore Favorite Action Memories

This exercise is adapted from Ogden and Fisher (2015).

1. Recall some of your most enjoyable activities from the past involving physical actions. Perhaps these are memories from your childhood or more recent times—playing games, fun, laughing, silliness, or pleasure might come to mind. (Some of my favorites are playing childhood games with friends like kick the can and red light/green light).

2. Pick two favorite action memories.

3. Describe them in writing or in your imagination. Recall images, sensations, emotions, and thoughts.

4. When you're finished, track sensations in your body, emotions, and your thoughts about yourself, others, and the world.

Recall Life's Accomplishments and Internal Resources

This exercise is adapted from Fouts (1990). A copy of this worksheet is also available at http://www.newharbinger .com/46646.

1. List *all* of your life's accomplishments, big and small. Don't forget to list the accomplishments from early in life, such as getting out of bed, separating from your parents to go to school, working hard, learning to ride a bike, showing kindness, or accommodating difficult family members. List anything that you felt was particularly difficult or that you received outside recognition for.

_____

_____

_____

_____

_____

_____

_____

_____

_____

_____

_____

_____

2. Next, begin to examine each accomplishment and list the qualities (the inner resources) it took to achieve that. Table 26.1 is a partial list of qualities that might stimulate your thinking. Please don't limit yourself to this list, but add others in the space provided if they are appropriate to the situation.

Table 26.1: List of Qualities

Artistry	Ambition	Creativity
Balance	Curiosity	Social Skills
Coordination	Risk Taking	Communication Skills
Memory	Courage	Empathy
Intelligence	Determination	Commitment
Compassion	Self-Discipline	Responsibility
Sense of Humor	Dependability	Loyalty
Negotiation Skills	Good Work Ethic	Hope
Assertiveness	Imagination	Intuition
Observation	Independence	Leadership
Cooperation or Teamwork	Respect	Integrity
Good Judgment	Perseverance	Calm Steadiness or Patience
Flexibility	Resilience	Enthusiasm
Others:		

For example, you might list accomplishments and qualities as follows:

Accomplishment	Qualities
Separated from parents and went to kindergarten	Independence, courage
Learned to ride a bike	Courage, memory, balance, coordination
Learned to dance in second grade	Social skills, courage, memory, balance, coordination

Use the following blank chart to organize your list:

Accomplishment	Qualities

3. You will find that certain qualities occur repeatedly throughout your list. Each time a quality is mentioned, place a check mark next to that quality in Table 26.1. Those qualities with the most check marks are the qualities that you've used more and are probably most comfortable with. They are your most effective tools to use when faced with difficult times. These qualities represent your greatest internal resources.

4. You may find that some qualities don't have many (or any) check marks. These may be qualities you have not had to use or qualities you'd like to improve. If you wish, circle the qualities on Table 26.1 that you'd like to gradually and joyfully develop. Remember that when you choose a quality to improve, it is not a criticism or an insult but reflects a healthy desire to grow. Any choice to make your life better is a *good thing*. This is what people with wholesome self-esteem do. Conversely, choosing to passively stagnate is choosing to give up on yourself and remain a victim of your past.

Anticipate Joy

Make a list of pleasures you anticipate experiencing tomorrow. Think about anything big or small—smiles, friends, something amusing or entertaining, nature, good food or drink, biking, spontaneously taking the kids out for ice cream, speaking to yourself kindly, a beautifully decorated room, and so on. Select two or three and envision for a few moments how it will feel emotionally and physically to experience these tomorrow.

Plan Pleasant Events

Make a list of things you used to do for fun that might still be enjoyable. Make a plan to do one each week for the next month. Given the link between the senses and memories, pay particular attention to what you see, hear, smell, taste, or feel against your skin as you do each pleasant event. This heightens the pleasure, while building a storehouse of pleasant memories that you can later recall. After doing each event, track how you feel emotionally and in your body.

Track Your Results

After trying the six joy exercises, select those that you favor. Try practicing each for three days or longer to reinforce the skill and to wire new neural circuits related to joy. Record your experience with each of the activities in your Skills Record (see appendix A).

CHAPTER 28

Create a New Future

Marcus Tullius Cicero long ago said, "Where there is life, there is hope." The life you've led doesn't have to be the life you lead. Though battered and bruised by ACEs, your core self is intact, and neuroplasticity enables you to rewire your brain in positive ways. You've probably noticed this growth occur as you've worked through this workbook. Keep going: be a builder of the future you want. If your caregivers have repeated harmful intergenerational patterns, know that you can be the transition person to change those patterns.

You can more and more become a joyful and resilient person—balancing your *past, present, and future.* You can be increasingly at peace with the *past*—having healed old wounds, rewired the brain, forgiven, and learned from your past experience, while remembering with pleasure the good times. (Healing is an ongoing process. Interestingly, as you heal old wounds, numbed emotions begin to thaw, restoring your capacity to feel and to remember with joy and other positive emotions.) You can have in mind a pleasant course for the *future*—without rigidly attaching to this plan. (Flexibility helps you avoid anger and disappointment when life throws you a curve.) Making peace with the past and having a direction for the future frees you to live contentedly in the *present.*

In this chapter, we'll explore three exercises to assist you in creating a new, bright future. They were inspired by master psychotherapists Pat Ogden and Francine Shapiro. Try each exercise one time, then continue to practice the exercises you find most effective to reinforce the new wiring in your brain.

Walk Through the Future Imagery

As curious as it seems, you can start by simply seeing yourself moving forward physically (Ogden and Fisher 2015).

1. Imagine yourself walking in the future. You are relaxed and poised.

2. Your feet land softly and gracefully as you walk. Your joints are loose, and your arms swing freely and with a smooth rhythm. Your spine is straight; your head is up. You feel energized and alert to all that is around you—all that is pleasant and all that requires caution. You feel strong and confident.

3. You feel secure in your human worth, which you know is equal to all your fellow human beings'. There's a bounce in your step. Life is good. You feel grateful for life with all its possibilities.

4. The next time you are walking outside, relax. Breathe. Try to walk this way and track what happens.

Inspired by Pat Ogden (Ogden and Fisher 2015) and Francine Shapiro (2012), this next exercise interrupts old negative patterns and creates new neural pathways. For example, you might rehearse new patterns in imagery for being a responsible, loving parent, partner, or friend. You might also consider this exercise for improving performance at work or play. A copy of this worksheet is also available at http://www.newharbinger.com/46646.

Create New Patterns

Find a comfortable position. Settle your mind in your breathing. Then answer the questions.

1. Describe a pattern you'd like to change. (For example, "I feel anxious in social settings.")

_____

_____

_____

_____

_____

2. Identify images, emotions, sensations, and thoughts that contribute to this pattern. (For example, "I see Dad's critical face. I feel scared. I assume people won't like me. My muscles tense and my shoulders tighten.")

_____

_____

_____

_____

_____

3. Mindfully respond. You calmly, confidently, and kindly simply name thoughts, emotions, sensations, and images as just that. (For example, you tell yourself, "There is fear—it's just a feeling; not who I am at the core. Feelings come and go. Whatever I feel is okay; let me feel it.") Write down your mindful responses.

    _____

    _____

    _____

    _____

    _____

    _____

4. Describe briefly how you would like to feel. (For example, "I'd like to feel calm and confident.")

    _____

    _____

    _____

    _____

    _____

    _____

5. Determine how you would like to respond. Direct your awareness to new images, emotions, sensations, and thoughts. (For example, "I feel kind and accepting of my fear. My body and my face are relaxed. I'm calm. My posture is graceful, confident, and welcoming. My face has a pleasant expression. With curious interest, I tune in to other people and notice their friendly expressions. I'm thinking that it's perfectly okay to be a bit uncomfortable; that's part of being human.")

    _____

    _____

    _____

    _____

    _____

6. Mentally rehearse. See yourself in the future responding to a challenging situation with this new pattern of images, sensations, emotions, and thoughts. You might adjust your posture to be consistent with your new feeling of confidence. You might also remind yourself, "This is a learning process. One step at a time. I bring kindness to this imperfect moment, and enjoy it." Write down any thoughts that come to mind.

_____

7. Practice this future imagery, with the new sensations, emotions, and thoughts, at least two more times. Make sure the imagery has a beginning, a middle, and an end. Then track the sensations in your body and emotions and see if they have shifted. Note these below.

_____

The following exercise encourages you to harness positive attachment relationships and carry these forward with you and draw comfort from them (Ogden and Fisher 2015). A copy of this worksheet is also available at http://www.newharbinger.com/46646.

Carry Resource Persons with You

1. Think about positive relationships you've had. Who comes to mind?

_____

2. Can you think of times when someone made you feel safe, secure, loved, protected, appreciated, or that you mattered? Describe those times and the people who made you feel that way. Describe the faces of these people. (Some of the same people may come to mind as did in step 1.)

_____

_____

_____

_____

_____

3. Select one of the people you've identified in step 1 or 2. Imagine that person in the room with you. Describe what you envision, and your emotions, bodily responses, and thoughts. Are there core thoughts that this person instilled that have made a positive difference (such as "I'm worthwhile; I'm lovable; I'm safe and protected")?

_____

_____

_____

_____

_____

4. During difficult times in the future, when you feel dysregulated, you know you can imagine that person being close to you as a resource. What would it be like to remember this person being with you during difficult times?

_____

_____

_____

_____

_____

Track Your Results

After trying these exercises, you might wish to select your favorites and practice them over the course of several days or longer. Record your experience with each of the activities in your Skills Record (see appendix A).

CHAPTER 29

Conclusion

Growth is a process. As you continue to heal and develop, you'll steadily become more secure in who you are. You'll feel a justifiable pride for surviving life's challenges thus far, and realize you are as worthwhile as anyone else. You'll feel authentic: the same person regardless of whom you are with, what you are doing, or what you are feeling. You'll value yourself and treat yourself accordingly. You'll honestly acknowledge your weaknesses as you recognize and gradually build your strengths. And you'll look to the future with optimism and good cheer.

I hope that this workbook has been a rich source of principles and skills that have helped you heal from the wounds of early life stress and rebuild a secure sense of self, which had been damaged by such experiences. Perhaps you've noticed that you've changed your relationship with pain and become more compassionate to yourself and others.

In working through this workbook, you've probably acquired a number of principles and skills that will continue to serve you throughout your lifetime. The challenge is to remember to use them. As a final exercise to solidify your progress, please flip through the entire workbook and record the ideas and skills you most want to remember. Your Skills Record will be a great resource in this process. The following exercise will help remind you of the tools you have at your disposal, especially during difficult times. A copy of this worksheet is also available at http://www.newharbinger.com /46646.

> *The most beautiful people we have known are those who have known defeat, known suffering, known struggle, known loss, and have found their way out of the depths. These persons have an appreciation, a sensitivity, and an understanding of life that fills them with compassion, gentleness, and a deep loving concern. Beautiful people do not just happen.*
>
> —Elisabeth Kübler-Ross

Record of Ideas and Skills

Ideas I Want to Remember

_____

_____

_____

_____

_____

_____

_____

_____

_____

_____

_____

_____

_____

_____

_____

_____

_____

Skills I Want to Remember

_____

_____

_____

_____

_____

_____

_____

_____

_____

_____

_____

_____

_____

_____

_____

_____

_____

_____

Skills Record

A copy of this worksheet is also available at http://www.newharbinger.com/46646. Or photocopy as needed.

Skill	Date	Time	Rate Effectiveness (from 0 to 10)		Comment
			Physical	Emotional	

Skill	Date	Time	Rate Effectiveness (from 0 to 10)		Comment
			Physical	Emotional	

Appendix A: Skills Record (continued)

Skill	Date	Time	Rate Effectiveness (from 0 to 10)		Comment
			Physical	Emotional	

Shame Symptoms Inventory

Shame, feeling bad to the core, can be imprinted implicitly or explicitly. People show shame in different ways, sometimes in surprising extremes that share much in common with insecure attachment. The following worksheet is adapted from Borysenko (1990), Bradshaw (1988), Flowers and Stahl (2011), Herman (2014), Potter-Efron and Potter-Efron (1989), Schore (2003), and Williams and Poijula (2013). A copy of this worksheet is also available at http://www.newharbinger.com/46646.

Without judging, check the items that describe you in general.

Overall Emotional State

_____   Fearful, even when relatively safe

_____   Negative (critical of self, others, or conditions; sarcastic)

_____   Irritable, angry, on guard

_____   Resentful, envious, wanting what others have that I lack

_____   Highly sensitive to criticism or rejection

_____   Easily overwhelmed

_____   Sad, shut down, collapsed, passive, frozen, stuck

Physical Signs

_____   Gaze aversion—downward gaze, avoiding eye contact, looking away when a painful topic comes up

_____   Stooped posture—head hangs down, shoulders slumped, bowed, inward curl from contracted psoas muscle; or the opposite: rigid, aggressive, hyperalert posture (shoulders hunch up)

_____ Hiding face with hands ("loss of face")

_____ Squirming, fidgeting

_____ Blushing

_____ Lips sucked in, corners down

_____ Licking lips, biting tongue

_____ Clenched jaw

_____ False smiles, nonhumorous laughing

_____ Furrowed brow

Somatic (Bodily) Changes

_____ Tingling

_____ Shivering

_____ Vibrating, trembling

_____ Dry throat

_____ Nausea

_____ Knotted gut

_____ Pressure or tightness in throat or chest

_____ Diarrhea or constipation

_____ Impulse to move or collapse

_____ Extremes in stress arousal—pounding heart, rapid breathing, high blood pressure might switch over time to slowing of heart or breathing, low blood pressure, no energy, feeling dead

Speech

_____ Soft speech, mumbling

_____ Fragmented speech

_____ Silences

_____   Stammering

_____   Hesitation, interrupting self

_____   Long pauses

_____   Confusion of thought

_____   Low, monotonous voice

Painful Feelings

_____   Self-loathing, self-contempt, self-dislike, low self-esteem

_____   Defiled, disgraced, dirty, dishonored, disrespected

_____   Disgusted with myself, my body, or sexual intimacy

_____   Inner pain or torment over shortcomings

_____   Lacking in self-respect

_____   Self-doubt

_____   Small, insignificant

_____   Inadequate

_____   Ridiculous, exposed, inferior to others

_____   Humiliation, wanting to hide from notice or sink under the floor

_____   Afraid that inadequacy will be discovered; worried about what others think

_____   Afraid of abandonment or rejection

_____   Afraid of intimacy

_____   Unlovable

_____   Helpless, powerless, hopeless

_____   Fragile

_____   Wrong

_____   Self-condemning

_____ Like a physical object

_____ Bad, unworthy

_____ Lonely, like I don't belong or fit in

_____ Ignored

_____ Confused

_____ Little delight or joy

_____ Unhappy (even though "successful"), overly serious, humorless

_____ Emotionally numb, hollow, empty, or flat

_____ Excessively guilty (for standing up for self, for mistakes, for disappointing others, and so on)

_____ Afraid of authority figures

_____ Suicidal (an understandable response when one knows no way to lessen intolerable pain)

Coping Behaviors. These logically follow from fears of evaluation, disappointment, or rejection.

To win acceptance, I tend to…

_____ Please people in order to not be rejected

_____ Smile to please people

_____ Apologize excessively

_____ Be overly submissive

_____ Avoid disagreeing with others

_____ Avoid standing up for myself or asserting my own preferences

_____ Seek others' approval to validate my uncertain worth

_____ Seek love and attention in unhealthy ways

_____ Attach to hurtful people to fulfill attachment needs

_____ Stay with hurtful people to defend against abandonment

_____   Act seductively

To hide my flawed self, I...

_____   Keep secrets (for example, I depict my family as normal; I don't talk about myself)

_____   Avoid people; am aloof, shy, isolated

_____   Hide from others, disappear from view

_____   Am unable to relax and let people know me

_____   Withdraw from relationships to spare myself from rejection

_____   Avoid challenges for fear of failing

_____   Am defensive, highly sensitive to criticism; deny wrongdoing

_____   Deny painful emotions (which prevents me from healing)

_____   Focus on fixing or controlling others, rather than loving and accepting myself

To fix myself (and possibly protect myself from rejection in the future), I...

_____   Am highly self-critical, harsh, or angry at myself (anger is less painful than shame)

_____   Am overly self-conscious and self-judging

_____   Notice only weaknesses in myself

To overcompensate (in order to escape the pain of shame), I...

_____   Put up a false front to impress others; don't accept my own imperfections

_____   Am arrogant, boastful

_____   Am narcissistic, grandiose, self-absorbed

_____   Consider myself invulnerable (an illusion)

_____   Show outward confidence to cover up a lack of confidence

_____   Try to fix myself (doggedly pursue perfection; relentlessly and without humor seek self-improvement, including plastic surgery, excessive fitness, driven pursuit of wealth or position)

_____ Am a super-achiever (for example, trying to be a supermom and putting pressure on the children to be perfect)

_____ Try to control everyone and everything

_____ Am overly orderly, clean

_____ Lie to spare disapproval of others

_____ Am defensive or overly aggressive ("a good offense is the best defense")

To hide or escape my own pain, I…

_____ Numb painful feelings (for example, through addictions, forgetting much of childhood, denying it hurts, dissociating)

_____ Am overly responsible for others to avoid looking within (codependence); I pity or rescue instead of love; I put others first despite the cost to myself

_____ Self-harm (consistent with self-dislike; opioids dull not only physical but also emotional pain from separation or rejection)

_____ Isolate myself from others

_____ Quit trying or give up so as not to feel the pain of failing

_____ Fight other people for the respect I don't feel for myself

_____ Try to avoid judgment from others by becoming invisible

_____ Please others so as not to risk disapproval

_____ Don't ask for what I prefer or need

_____ Try to be perfect to win approval

_____ Deny blame for doing something wrong

To project my own pain onto others (attacking others to feel superior and to counter feelings of insignificance), I tend to…

_____ Blame others and assume the victim role (this also avoids responsibility)

_____ Be destructive, wanting to strike back for lost face; lash out in pain, rage, or fury

_____ Criticize others

Lack of Self-Care (which logically follows from feelings of little self-worth)

_____   I neglect or ignore my own needs.

_____   I sabotage, abuse, or harm myself.

_____   I give in to addictions or other temporary distractions, such as excitement, drugs, empty sex.

_____   I remain in bad relationships—allow others to mistreat me, cling to bad relationships for fear of abandonment.

Schema (deeply held views or felt sense that tends to drive many of the above symptoms)

_____   I don't belong in the world; I don't fit in.

_____   I'm a black sheep in the family.

_____   Something is basically wrong/bad with me.

_____   I'm defective, weak, disgusting, despicable, dirty.

_____   I'm too flawed to be loved.

_____   I'm inept, inadequate.

_____   People will tolerate but not embrace me.

_____   I'm unlovable (that's why they left me).

_____   Others are more worthwhile than I am.

_____   I'll never get it right.

_____   I'm either in control, perfect, a superstar, or I'm worthless.

_____   I'm flawed to the core and that's awful.

_____   I'm a disappointment to those who matter, including myself.

_____   I'm no good, or not good enough.

_____   I'm a failure (a gnawing, unsettled feeling that persists despite outward successes).

_____   Bad things happen to bad people. Since bad things happened to me, I'm a bad person.

_____   It's awful to be criticized.

_____   My parent was a bum. I'm his or her offspring, so I'm a bum.

_____   My feelings, thoughts, or desires don't matter to anyone.

_____   My feelings hurt too much to acknowledge. It's better to numb them out.

_____   I'm completely to blame for all that is wrong in my life.

_____   I'll improve if I harshly criticize or beat myself up.

_____   I'm trash beside the road.

_____   I don't deserve to succeed, live a good life, or perhaps even live at all.

_____   I'm an imposter.

_____   I must not take any risks.

Spiritual Despair

_____   I wonder, "Where do I stand before God? Will God forsake me? Am I irredeemable?"

_____   I feel cut off from God and others.

_____   I feel that innocence has been lost and can't be regained.

_____   I don't feel God's presence/closeness/love; I feel that I can't approach or collaborate with God.

_____   I feel disconnected from comfort, peace, and protecting power.

_____   I feel unclean and unforgivable.

Acknowledgments

In writing this workbook, I've truly felt as though I've stood on the shoulders of giants. First and foremost, I recognize Dr. Vincent Felitti, who (with colleague Dr. Robert Anda) conceived the ACEs Study and has tirelessly worked to raise awareness of the link between ACEs and health outcomes. I also acknowledge Jane Stevens, who is indefatigable in educating the world about ACEs and healing through the ACEs Connection Network. Despite an enormous workload, she and her staff somehow maintain a friendly, personal touch in their work. In addition, thanks to Dr. Nadine Burke Harris, who, from a public health perspective, has so tirelessly addressed the need to confront ACEs.

I've been greatly influenced by Dr. Allan Schore, whose long career of patient, diligent research linking attachment psychology to developmental neuroscience has significantly furthered the germinal work of attachment pioneers Drs. John Bowlby and Mary Ainsworth.

Dr. Pat Ogden has made invaluable contributions in healing traumatic wounds with body-based treatments—the missing piece of the trauma puzzle. I'm especially grateful to her influence related to the skills in regulating stress arousal, changing shame programming, and (along with the late Dr. Francine Shapiro) creating a new future.

I'm grateful for the many who have inspired the imagery exercises in this workbook, including Drs. Henry Cloud, Daniel Siegel, Kent Hoffman, Alicia Lieberman, Clancy McKenzie, Ruth Newton, and Allan Schore; and especially April Steele, MSc, for her brilliant work with self-nurturing imagery.

I gratefully acknowledge Dr. William Zangwill, who originated the important floatback strategies, and Cindy Browning, LCSW, and Dr. Francine Shapiro, who further developed them.

I appreciate the idea of putting inadequacies into perspective, as suggested by Dr. Wendy Ulrich and developed in chapter 28.

Tesilya Hanauer and the other editorial and production staff at New Harbinger Publications have provided such patient and consistent encouragement and caring support. Thank you!

Those who have survived ACEs and other forms of trauma constantly inspire me. Thank you for your courage and perseverance as you strive to overcome your difficult times. Thank you for helping me learn, as we've worked together, how to better strengthen and support you. I am a better person for knowing you.

Last and certainly not least, deep and special thanks go to my wife, Dori, for being such a consummate secure and loving attachment figure to the children and me.

Recommended Resources

Adverse Childhood Experiences (ACEs)

ACEs Connection Network. Jane Stevens, founder and publisher (jstevens@acesconnection.com). Supports communities to accelerate the use of ACEs science to solve our most intractable problems through:

> ACEs Connection (ACEsConnection.com). A worldwide social network that unites tens of thousands of people and thousands of organizations, systems, and communities interested in understanding, preventing, and healing from ACEs. As the ACEs movement's main information exchange and resource, it supports hundreds of local ACEs initiatives around the world with tools and guidelines to grow their initiatives. At this site, you'll find news, scientific information, research, trauma-informed and resilience-building practices and policies, resources, and ACEs surveys.

> ACEs Too High (ACEsTooHigh.com). News site distributes news about ACEs science, research, reports, and latest developments, as well as how different sectors—such as education, health care, law enforcement, and faith-based communities—are integrating trauma-informed practices based on ACEs science.

Post-Traumatic Stress Disorder (PTSD)

Finding Specialized Trauma Treatment

Adults who understand and have resolved their traumatic wounds suffer less and are better able to form more secure attachments with their children.

Accelerated Resolution Therapy (ART; Orlando, FL; 877-675-7153; https://acceleratedresolutiontherapy .com). ART is a promising treatment using eye movements that erases old disturbing images and replaces them with positive ones. Go to their website to find an ART therapist.

EMDR Institute (831-761-1040; https://www.emdr.com). International directory of EMDR-trained clinicians.

EMDR International Association (Austin, TX; 866-451-5200; https://www.emdria.org). This site can help you find an EMDR therapist.

GoodTherapy.org. Search by location and specialty area for therapists, who introduce themselves and describe fees and insurance coverage.

HelpPRO Therapist Finder (781-862-5215; https://www.helppro.com). Find a local therapist who identifies as a trauma therapist.

Intensive Trauma Therapy (304-291-2912; https://www.TraumaTherapy.us). Locate a therapist trained in the Instinctual Trauma Response™ treatment method, which helps one settle and complete the trauma story in a relatively quick and well-tolerated way. Also trains parents, educators, and therapists (www. ITRtraining.com).

International Society for Traumatic Stress Studies (847-686-2234; https://istss.org). Find trauma clinicians in your area.

National Child Traumatic Stress Network (919-682-1552; nctsn.org). Diverse resources for traumatized children, their families, and mental health professionals. Send email to info@nctsn.org to request local centers providing clinical care for traumatized children and their families. For additional ways to find professional mental health assistance, click the "GET HELP NOW" button on the homepage and then "Seeking Mental Health Guidance and Referrals." The website also provides written and video resources on trauma, attachment, and trauma treatments and their effectiveness. Also, it offers education and training for trauma professionals.

Sensorimotor Psychotherapy Institute (800-860-9258; https://www.sensorimotorpsychotherapy.org). Find local therapists practicing Dr. Pat Ogden's sensorimotor therapy.

SIDRAN Institute (Derwood, MD; 410-825-8888; https://help@sidran.org; https:// www.sidran.org). Provides names of local trauma specialists, readings, and other resources.

About Trauma Treatments

Schiraldi, G. R. 2016. *The Post-Traumatic Stress Disorder Sourcebook*. New York: McGraw-Hill. Clearly explains the nature and diverse treatments of post-traumatic stress disorder, which can result from adversities ranging from ACEs to combat and rape.

Shapiro, R. 2010. *The Trauma Treatment Handbook*. New York: W. W. Norton. Another good overview of the various treatments for traumatic stress.

Courtois, C. A., and Ford, J. D. 2013. *Treatment of Complex Trauma: A Sequenced, Relationship-Based Approach*. New York: Guilford. Single or short treatment modalities are often insufficient for those exposed to early, severe, recurring childhood abuse and neglect.

Body-Oriented Treatments

Emotional Freedom Technique (https://www.emofree.com). Good for calming; can be useful when EMDR stalls. Protocol is free on the website.

Levine, P. A. 2010. *In an Unspoken Voice: How the Body Releases Trauma and Restores Goodness.* Berkeley, CA: North Atlantic Books. Levine's Somatic Experiencing® provides an approach to helping survivors sense trauma in the body and release the locked energy in a titrated way. Also see Levine, P. A., and Kline, M. (2008). *Trauma-Proofing Your Kids.* Berkeley, CA: North Atlantic Books.

Miller-Karas, E. 2015. *Building Resilience to Trauma: The Trauma and Community Resiliency Models.* New York: Routledge. Practical body-based interventions for clinicians and laypersons. Also, go to https://www.traumaresourceinstitute.com for the free iChill app, which teaches very useful self-help body-based skills to return to the resilient zone, such as tracking, resourcing, and first aid for difficult times.

Ogden, P., K. Minton, and C. Pain. 2006. *Trauma and the Body: A Sensorimotor Approach to Psychotherapy.* New York: W. W. Norton. On the forefront of body-oriented therapies, Ogden presents an integrated approach to healing trauma that integrates cognition, emotions, and the body. When top-down (cognitive) approaches don't work, Ogden offers bottom-up alternatives. See also the companion workbook: Ogden, P., and J. Fisher. 2015. *Sensorimotor Psychotherapy: Interventions for Trauma and Attachment.* New York: W. W. Norton.

Note: You might ask about other well-researched trauma treatments, such as cognitive processing therapy, prolonged exposure, and individual cognitive behavioral therapy with a trauma focus. Ask prospective therapists about their experience treating childhood trauma, sometimes called complex or developmental trauma. Also, emerging evidence indicates that self-guided internet-based interventions for trauma might be useful for some people.

Imaginal Nurturing

Steele, A. 2007. *Developing a Secure Self: An Attachment-Based Approach to Adult Psychotherapy.* CDs and printed guide. Gabriola, BC, Canada: April Steele (https://april-steele.ca). Powerful imagery exercises to address attachment deficits and self-esteem related to the early years, and to complement trauma work. The imagined infant represents the core of who you are as an individual. Exercises aim to develop a new relationship with yourself, a relationship perhaps damaged in the early years, as well as to separate the past from the present, and/or prepare for trauma work by strengthening the individual and promoting confidence to explore. Simple and safe with no apparent harmful side effects.

Attachment-Based Couples and Family Therapy

Emotion-focused therapy for couples (EFT; www.iceeft.com). When attachment insecurities are interfering with intimate relationships, EFT therapists help you uncover vulnerabilities that you are not fully aware of and address underlying emotional issues in a way that strengthens attachment bonds. Based on the work of Susan Johnson (2019). Partners are guided to address and heal attachment injuries through soothing and supportive responses. More effective than building traditional couples skills; over 70 percent of couples find their relationship permanently improves. At the core is an honest expression of attachment needs and working together to create a safe haven and secure base. Johnson has also developed emotionally focused family therapy (EFFT).

Stress and Trauma Release Exercises

Berceli, D. 2015. *Shake It Off Naturally: Reduce Stress, Anxiety, and Tension with Trauma Release Exercises* (TRE). DVD, 40 minutes. The psoas muscle connects the lower spine to the pelvis and femur. It instinctively contracts when we flinch in response to a threat or prepare to fight or flee. Seven easy-to-learn exercises help this major muscle release unnoticed tension that is stuck in traumatic memories, including sexual abuse, as the brain is still trying to help the person survive. This chronic tension often causes pain in the back, shoulders, and neck, along with gastrointestinal problems. Allowing natural shaking/tremors to occur is usually calming. Useful as self-help to reduce stress or as an adjunct to other trauma modalities. Exercises take about 15 minutes.

Ping Shuai Gong—Swing Hands Exercise (English; YouTube video from Master Li Feng Shan; 33 minutes). A very relaxing and energizing practice to regulate the body.

Nutritional Brain Care

Oldways (http://tiny.cc/8jspzy). A respected nonprofit for improving health through nutrition. Find Mediterranean meal plans.

Relevant Reads

Neff, K. 2011. *Self-Compassion: The Proven Power of Being Kind to Yourself.* New York: William Morrow. Self-compassion is central to healing from ACEs. Also go to https://self-compassion.org for self-compassion self-assessment and other useful tools.

Schiraldi, G. R. 2016. *The Self-Esteem Workbook*. Oakland, CA: New Harbinger. Skills to build wholesome self-esteem, which helps prevent and facilitate recovery from stress-related disorders. An important complement to this workbook, because ACEs typically damage self-esteem.

Schiraldi, G. R. 2017. *The Resilience Workbook*. Oakland, CA: New Harbinger. A range of skills to recover from adversity and optimize mental health and performance. Resilience has been found to be an effective countermeasure to ACEs.

Shapiro, F. 2012. *Getting Past Your Past*. New York: Rodale. From the originator of EMDR, many useful principles and skills to heal from past adversities.

Joint Trauma Treatments for Children, Adolescents, and Caregivers

Child Parent Psychotherapy (CPP; https://childparentpsychotherapy.com). Based on attachment theory, helps child from birth to five years and parent/caregiver heal. Children and parents are treated as a team, because children need parents around them. Helps children with trauma or mental health, attachment, or behavioral problems. Helps child and parents understand what they experienced and jointly construct a trauma story. Parents learn how their own trauma affects their parenting. Play therapy helps the child communicate. Many skills help both child and parent cope and bond. This early life intervention helps break intergenerational transmission of trauma. Usually fifty-two weekly sessions in home or office playroom.

Parent Child Interaction Therapy (PCIT; https://pcit.ucdavis.edu; pcit.org). For children with behavioral problems and autism and for adoptive/foster families. Builds relationship and child management skills through parent/child coaching sessions. Usually twelve to twenty sessions.

Trauma-Focused Cognitive Behavioral Therapy (TF-CBT; https://tfcbt.org). Well researched in many countries. Helps children and adolescents aged three to eighteen recover from single, multiple, and complex trauma, as well as depression, anxiety, and behavioral problems. Most show significant improvement within sixteen sessions, which include individual child and parent sessions as well as joint sessions with nonoffending parent/caregiver. Components include parenting skills, managing stress and emotions, trauma processing, telling the trauma story, replacing harmful thoughts, real-life exposure to triggers that are no longer dangerous, and future strategies for preventing self-injury, coping with suicidal thoughts, and building relationships.

Parents, Children, and Community

Parenting Support

Circle of Security (509-462-2024; https://www.circleofsecurityinternational.com). Early intervention program for parents. Eight- or twenty-week programs help strengthen parent–child relationships and raise a secure child. Provides parents with a model of secure relationships and videos of parent–child interactions. Parents learn to regulate their emotions in response to child's distress, read child's emotional needs, help child manage emotions, and enhance child's self-esteem.

Home-visiting child abuse/neglect prevention programs. Parents, including expecting mothers, are visited in the home, where they receive education in effective parenting, help accessing social support and community services, or help obtaining education and employment. Examples:

- Attachment and Biobehavioral Catch-up (302-831-0534; www.abcintervention.org). Promotes infant–caregiver attachment security and self-regulation. Ten weekly one-hour home visits provide caregivers of infants and toddlers who have experienced early adversity positive feedback of videotaped interactions. Program has been found to benefit both child and caregiver.

- Child First (203-538-5222; https://www.childfirst.org). Free intensive home-based services help very vulnerable young children (prenatal through five years) and families heal from the effects of trauma and adversity. Weekly visits empower parents to create a stable and nurturing home. Connects families to needed community services, and builds strong and loving parent–child relationships. Helps parents find a job, safe place to live, speech therapist, and medical services.

- Head Start and Early Head Start (866-763-6481; https://www.acf.hhs.gov). Free federally funded community-based program for low-income families with pregnant women, infants, toddlers, or children up to age five. Links families to needed services and provides home visits and safe environments for children.

- Healthy Families America (312-663-3520; https://www.healthyfamiliesamerica.org). Regular home visits for parents facing challenges such as single parenthood, low income, a history of ACEs, or substance abuse. Families enroll prenatally or within three months of a child's birth and receive services through child's fifth birthday. Many sites offer parent support groups and father involvement programs.

- Nurse-Family Partnership (844-637-6667; https://www.nursefamilypartnership.org). Find a free personal nurse for home visits to first-time moms who live in poverty across the US (dads can join in). Nurse offers advice and support from pregnancy until the child is two.

National Center for Fathering (913-222-9494; fathers.com). Nonprofit shares research and education for equipping fathers and father figures to engage in the lives of every child. Free weekly newsletter provides ideas, advice, and inspiration.

National Parent Helpline (855-427-2736; www.nationalparenthelpline.org). Emotional support from a trained advocate. Directs you to a wide range of parenting resources.

SAFE® Secure Attachment Family Education (https://www.khbrisch.de/en/prevention-projects/safe). Parenting group promotes secure attachment between parents and child. Four modules from pregnancy to end of first year. Expectant parents examine trauma from their own childhoods and explore expectations for when baby arrives, parenting skills, fantasies and fears, and stress reduction. Other topics include the birthing experience, postpartum depression, nursing, sleep, observation of parent–child attachment, recognizing and responding appropriately to baby's signals, what to do when baby won't sleep or be consoled, and treatment of unresolved trauma in parents. Available in Europe, US, Russia, Australia, and New Zealand.

Fee-Based Parenting Education

Incredible Years (206-285-7565; www.incredibleyears.com). Evidence-based group programs for parents, children, and teachers aim to prevent and manage young children's behavior problems (for example, related to ADHD, autism, conduct problems) and promote social, emotional, and academic competence. Often providers are supported by external funding, thus minimizing cost.

Triple P Online (https://www.triplep-parenting.com). Online parenting program lets you choose strategies that fit your family's needs.

Teaching Children Empathy

B.A.S.E.® Babywatching (https://www.base-babywatching.de/en). Helps children ages three to twelve develop emotional health and prepare for adulthood by developing sensitivity and empathy, growing attachment capacities, and countering fear and aggression. Children observe a parent and infant once a week over the first year of the baby's life. They describe what the parent and baby are doing and why, and how the two interact and influence each other emotionally. Finally, the children are asked how they feel as they imagine themselves in the position of the parent or baby. Research shows participating children become less aggressive, oppositional, anxious, depressed, withdrawing, and hyperactive and experience fewer physical symptoms in girls and fewer sleep disorders. Implemented in daycare centers, schools, correctional, and trauma inpatient settings. Parents, teachers, and elderly also benefit from the positive emotional experience.

For Schools

Empowering Education (https://empoweringeducation.org). Comprehensive mindfulness-based social and emotional learning. Teaches coping skills, solving problems peacefully, breathing, self-compassion, wholesome self-talk, and cooperation.

Helping Traumatized Children Learn (https://traumasensitiveschools.org). Recognizes trauma as a cause of learning problems; safe and supportive schools.

Peacemaker Resources (218-444-8048; https://www.peacemakerresources.org). Training to schools and youth organizations on social and emotional skills.

For Professionals

SAFE® Secure Attachment Family Education (https://www.safe-programm.de/en). Works with professionals who work with pregnant mothers, parents, and their infants.

Zero to Three (800-899-4301; https://www.zerotothree.org). Provides professionals working with children (or working with those who teach others to deal with children) with resources on total child development in the first three years of life.

Also see National Child Traumatic Stress Network above.

References

Allen, J. G., L. Coyne, and J. Huntoon. 1998. "Complex Posttraumatic Stress Disorder in Women from a Psychometric Perspective." *Journal of Personality Assessment* 70: 277–298.

Annand, K. J. S., and P. R. Hickey. 1987. "Pain and Its Effects in the Human Neonate and Fetus." *The New England Journal of Medicine* 317: 1321–1329.

Ano, G. G., and E. B. Vasconcelles. 2005. "Religious Coping and Psychological Adjustment to Stress: A Meta-Analysis." *Journal of Clinical Psychology* 61: 461–480.

Anonymous Press. 1992. *Mini Edition of AA.* Malo, WA: The Anonymous Press.

Askelund, A. D., S. Schweizer, I. M. Goodyer, and A.-L. van Harmelen. 2019. "Positive Memory Specificity Is Associated with Reduced Vulnerability to Depression." *Nature Human Behaviour* 3: 265–273.

Bandelow, B., C. Späth, G. A. Tichauer, A. Broocks, G. Hajak, and E. Rüther. 2002. "Early Traumatic Life Events, Parental Attitudes, Family History, and Birth Risk Factors in Patients with Panic Disorder." *Comprehensive Psychiatry* 43: 269–278.

Bandelow, B., A. Charimo Torrente, D. Wedekind, A. Broocks, G. Hajak, and E. Rüther. 2004. "Early Traumatic Life Events, Parental Rearing Styles, Family History of Mental Disorders, and Birth Risk Factors in Patients with Social Anxiety Disorder." *European Archives of Psychiatry and Clinical Neuroscience* 254: 397–405.

Berlin, L. J., J. Cassidy, and K. Appleyard. 2008. "The Influence of Early Attachments on Other Relationships." In *Handbook of Attachment*, 2nd ed., edited by J. Cassidy and P. R. Shaver. New York: Guilford.

Blumenthal, J. A., P. J. Smith, S. Mabe, A. Hinderliter, P. Lin, L. Liao, et al. 2019. "Lifestyle and Neurocognition in Older Adults with Cognitive Impairments: A Rondomized Trial." *Neurology* 92: e212–e223.

Borysenko, J. 1990. *Guilt Is the Teacher, Love Is the Lesson.* New York: Hachette Book Group.

Bradshaw, J. 1988. *Healing the Shame That Binds You.* Deerfield Beach, FL: Health Communications.

Bray, R. L. 2017. "Thought Field Therapy Center of San Diego." /rlbray.com.

Brisch, K. H. 2011. *Treating Attachment Disorders: From Theory to Therapy.* 2nd ed. New York: Guilford.

Brooks, A. 2008. *Gross National Happiness: Why Happiness Matters for America—and How We Can Get More of It.* New York: Basic Books.

Browning, C. 1999. "Floatback and Float Forward: Techniques for Linking Past, Present and Future." *EMDRIA Newsletter* 4: 12–13.

Cassidy, J. 2008. "The Nature of the Child's Ties." In *Handbook of Attachment: Theory, Research, and Clinical Applications,* 2nd ed., edited by J. Cassidy and P. R. Shaver. New York: Guilford.

Cerci, D., and E. Colucci. 2017. "Forgiveness in PTSD After Man-Made Traumatic Events: A Systematic Review." *Traumatology* 24: 47–54.

Chen, Y., and T. J. VanderWeele. 2018. "Associations of Religious Upbringing with Subsequent Health and Well-being from Adolescence to Young Adulthood: An Outcome-wide Analysis." *American Journal of Epidemiology* 187: 2355–2364.

Childre, D. L., and D. Rozman. 2005. *Transforming Stress: The HeartMath Solution for Relieving Worry, Fatigue, and Tension.* Oakland, CA: New Harbinger Publications.

Craig, G. 2013. "The EFT Basic Recipe by Founder Gary Craig." www.youtube.com/watch?v=1wG2FA4vfLQ.

Currier, J. M., J. M. Holland, and K. D. Drescher. 2015. "Spirituality Factors in the Prediction of Outcomes of PTSD Treatment for U. S. Military Veterans." *Journal of Traumatic Stress* 28: 57–64.

Davidson, R. J. 2009. Keynote address at Investigating and Integrating Mindfulness in Medicine, Health Care, and Society conference, Worcester, MA.

Eidhof, M. B., A. A. A. M. J. Djelantik, E. R. Klaassens, V. Kantor, D. Rittmansberger, M. Sleijpen, et al. 2019. "Complex Posttraumatic Stress Disorder in Patients Exposed to Emotional Neglect and Traumatic Events: Latent Class Analysis." *Journal of Traumatic Stress* 32: 23–31.

Emerson, R. W. 1901. "The American Scholar," an oration delivered before Harvard's Phi Beta Kappa Society, August 31, 1837. New York: Laurentian Press.

Engel, B. 2006. *Healing Your Emotional Self*. New York: Wiley.

Enright, R. 2012. *The Forgiving Life: A Pathway to Overcoming Resentment and Creating a Legacy of Love*. Washington, DC: American Psychological Association.

Epstein, L. J. 2010. "The Surprising Toll of Sleep Deprivation." *Newsweek*, June 28 and July 5, 75.

Farnsworth, J. K., and K. W. Sewell. 2011. "Fear of Emotion as a Moderator Between PTSD and Firefighter Social Interactions." *Journal of Traumatic Stress* 24: 444–450.

Farrell, W., and J. Gray. 2018. *The Boy Crisis: Why Our Boys Are Struggling and What We Can Do About It*. Dallas, TX: BenBella Books.

Felitti, V. 2002. "The Relation Between Adverse Childhood Experiences and Adult Health: Turning Gold into Lead." *Permanente Journal* 6: 44–47.

Felitti, V., and R. F. Anda. 2014. "The Lifelong Effects of Adverse Childhood Experiences." In *Child Maltreatment: Sexual Abuse and Psychological Maltreatment*, vol. 2, 4th ed., edited by D. L. Chadwick et al. St. Louis: STM Learning.

Figley, C. R. 1995. Correspondence to colleagues in traumatic stress. June 27.

Flowers, S., and B. Stahl. 2011. *Living with Your Heart Wide Open: How Mindfulness and Compassion Can Free You from Unworthiness, Inadequacy, and Shame*. Oakland, CA: New Harbinger Publications.

Foa, E. B., A. Ehlers, D. M. Clark, D. F. Tolin, and S. M. Orsillo. 1999. "The Posttraumatic Cognitions Inventory (PTCI): Development and Validation." *Psychological Assessment* 11: 303–314.

Follette, V. M., and J. Pistorello. 2007. *Finding Life Beyond Trauma: Using Acceptance and Commitment Therapy to Heal from Post-Traumatic Stress and Trauma-Related Problems*. Oakland, CA: New Harbinger Publications.

Fouts, J. D. 1990. "Life's Accomplishments and Internal Resources." Handout.

Francis, H. M., R. J. Stevenson, J. R. Chambers, D. Gupta, B. Newey, and C. K. Lim. 2019. "A Brief Diet Intervention Can Reduce Symptoms of Depression in Young Adults—A Randomised Controlled Trial." *PLoS One* 14: e0222768.

George, C., N. Kaplan, and M. Main. 1985. *Adult Attachment Interview Protocol*, 2nd ed. Unpublished manuscript, Department of Psychology, University of California, Berkeley.

Gilbert, P., and S. Procter. 2006. "Compassionate Mind Training for People with High Shame and Self-Criticism: Overview and Pilot Study of a Group Therapy Approach." *Clinical Psychology and Psychotherapy* 13: 353–379.

Goddard, A. W. 2017. "The Neurobiology of Panic: A Chronic Stress Disorder." *Chronic Stress* 1: 1–14.

Granqvist, P., T. Ivarsson, A. G. Broberg, and B. Hagekull. 2007. "Examining Relations Among Attachment, Religiosity, and New Age Spirituality Using the Adult Attachment Interview." *Developmental Psychology* 43: 590–601.

Grossman, K., K. E. Grossman, H. Kindler, and P. Zimmermann. 2008. "A Wider View of Attachment and Exploration: The Influence of Mothers and Fathers on the Development of Psychological Security from Infancy to

Young Adulthood." In *Handbook of Attachment: Theory, Research, and Clinical Applications*, 2nd ed., edited by J. Cassidy and P. R. Shaver. New York: Guilford.

Hammermeister, J. J., and M. Peterson. 2001. "Does Spirituality Make a Difference? Psychosocial and Health-Related Characteristics of Spiritual Well-Being." *American Journal of Health Education* 32: 293–297.

Harrison, C. C. 2012. *He Did Deliver Me from Bondage*. Hyrum, UT: Hearthaven Publishing.

Harvard University. Center on the Developing Child. N.D. https://developingchild.harvard.edu.

Harvey, S. T., and J. E. Taylor. 2010 "A Meta-Analysis of the Effects of Psychotherapy with Sexually Abused Children and Adolescents." *Clinical Psychology Review* 30: 517–535.

Haug, W., and P. Wanner. 2000. "The Demographic Characteristics of Linguistic and Religious Groups in Switzerland." In *The Demographic Characteristics of National Minorities in Certain European States*, vol. 2, edited by W. Haug, P. Compton, and Y. Courbage.

Hayes, S. C., with S. Smith. 2005. *Get Out of Your Mind and Into Your Life: The New Acceptance and Commitment Therapy*. Oakland, CA: New Harbinger Publications.

Hayes, S. C., K. D. Strosahl, and K. G. Wilson. 1999. *ACT: An Experiential Approach to Behavior Change*. New York: Guilford.

Heller, L., and A. LaPierre. 2012. *Healing Developmental Trauma: How Early Trauma Affects Self-Regulation, Self-Image, and the Capacity for Relationship*. Berkeley, CA: North Atlantic Books.

Hendel, H. J. 2018. *It's Not Always Depression*. London: Penguin Life.

Herman, J. L. 2014. "PTSD as a Shame Disorder: A Work in Progress." ISTSS Webinar. October 15. jherman@challiance.org. https://www.istss.org/ISTSS_Main/media/Webinar_Recordings/WEB1014/slides.pdf.

Hoeppner, B. B., M. R. Schick, H. Carlon, and S. S. Hoeppner. 2019. "Do Self-Administered Positive Psychology Exercises Work in Persons in Recovery from Problematic Substance Use? An Online Randomized Survey." *Journal of Substance Abuse Treatment* 99: 16–23.

Huttunen, M. O., and P. Niskanen. 1978. "Prenatal Loss of Father and Psychiatric Disorders." *Archives of General Psychiatry* 35: 429–431.

Huuskes, L. M., P. C. L. Heaven, J. Ciarrochi, P. Parker, and N. Caltabiano. 2016. "Is Belief in God Related to Differences in Adolescents' Psychological Functioning?" *Journal for the Scientific Study of Religion* 55: 40–53.

Imrie, S., and N. A. Troop. 2012. "A Pilot Study of the Effects and Feasibility of Compassion-Focused Expressive Writing in Day Hospice Patients." *Palliative & Supportive Care* 10: 115–122.

Johnson, S. M. 2019. *Attachment Theory in Practice: Emotionally Focused Therapy (EFT) with Individuals, Couples, and Families*. New York: Guilford.

Karen, R. 1994. *Becoming Attached: First Relationships and How They Shape Our Capacity to Love*. New York: Oxford University Press.

Kaufman, G. 1996. *The Psychology of Shame*, 2nd ed. New York: Springer Publishing.

Kearney, D. J., C. A. Malte, C. McManus, M. E. Martinex, B. Felleman, and T. L. Simpson. 2013. "Loving-kindness Meditation for Posttraumatic Stress Disorder: A Pilot Study." *Journal of Traumatic Stress* 26: 426–434.

Kendrick, S., and A. Kendrick. 2011. *The Resolution for Men*. Nashville: B&H Publishing.

Kirschbaum, C., J. C. Prüssner, A. A. Stone, I. Federenko, J. Gaab, D. Lintz, et al. 1995. "Persistent High Cortisol Responses to Repeated Psychological Stress in a Subpopulation of Healthy Men." *Psychosomatic Medicine* 57: 468–474.

Koenig, H. G. 1997. *Is Religion Good for Your Health? The Effects of Religion on Physical and Mental Health*. New York: Hayworth Pastoral Press.

Koenig, H. G. 2012. "Religion, Spirituality, and Health: The Research and Clinical Implications." *International Scholarly Research Network Psychiatry* 2012: 278730.

Koenig, H., D. E. King, and V. B. Carson. 2012. *Handbook of Religion and Health*, 2nd ed. New York: Oxford University Press.

Levine, P. A. 2010. *In an Unspoken Voice: How the Body Releases Trauma and Restores Goodness*. Berkeley, CA: North Atlantic Books.

Levy-Shiff, R., M. A. Hoffman, S. Mogilner, S. Levinger, and M. B. Mogilner. 1990. "Fathers' Hospital Visits to Their Preterm Infants as a Predictor of Father-Infant Relationship and Infant Development." *Pediatrics* 86: 289–293.

Lewis, T., F. Amini, and R. Lannon. 2000. *A General Theory of Love*. New York: Vintage.

Lipsitt, L. P. 2012. "Long-term Consequences of Perinatal Trauma." In *Encyclopedia of Trauma: An Interdisciplinary Guide*, edited by C. R. Figley. Thousand Oaks, CA: Sage.

Litz, B. T., L. Lebowitz, M. J. Gray, and W. P. Nash. 2016. *Adaptive Disclosure: A New Treatment for Military Trauma, Loss, and Moral Injury*. New York: Guilford.

Maslow, A. 1968. *Toward a Psychology of Being*, 2nd ed. New York: Van Nostrand Reinhold.

McEwen, B. S. 2017. "Neurobiological and Systemic Effects of Chronic Stress." *Chronic Stress (Thousand Oaks)* 1. doi:10.1177/2470547017692328.

McKenzie, C. D., and L. S. Wright. 1996. *Delayed Posttraumatic Stress Disorders from Infancy: The Two Trauma Mechanism*. New York: Taylor & Francis.

Meewisse, M., M. Olff, R. Kleber, N. J. Kitchiner, and B. P. R. Gersons. 2011. "The Course of Mental Health Disorders After a Disaster: Predictors and Comorbidity." *Journal of Traumatic Stress* 24: 405–413.

Mellin, L. 2010. *Wired for Joy: A Revolutionary Method for Creating Happiness from Within*. New York: Hay House.

Michigan Department of Health and Human Services (DHHS). 2017. Pub. 806. "Fatherhood: Give your Child the Dadvantage." https://www.michigan.gov/childsupport.

Mikulincer, M., and P. R. Shaver. 2008. "Adult Attachment and Affect Regulation." In *Handbook of Attachment*, 2nd ed., edited by J. Cassidy and P. R. Shaver. New York: Guilford.

Miller-Karas, E. 2015. *Building Resilience to Trauma: The Trauma and Community Resiliency Model*. New York: Routledge.

Nakazawa, D. J. 2015. *Childhood Disrupted: How Your Biography Becomes Your Biology, and How You can Heal*. New York: Atria.

Nakazawa, D.J. 2020. *The Angel and the Assassin: The Tiny Brain Cell that Changed the Course of Medicine*. New York: Ballantine.

Neff, K. 2011. *Self-Compassion: The Proven Power of Being Kind to Yourself*. New York: William Morrow.

Newberg, A., and M. R. Waldman. 2009. *How God Changes Your Brain: Breakthrough Findings from a Leading Neuroscientist*. New York: Ballantine.

Ogden, P., and J. Fisher. 2015. *Sensorimotor Psychotherapy: Interventions for Trauma and Attachment*. New York: W. W. Norton.

Ogden, P., K. Minton, and C. Pain. 2006. *Trauma and the Body: A Sensorimotor Approach to Psychotherapy*. New York: W. W. Norton.

Pelletier, K. R. 2019. *Change Your Genes, Change Your Life*. San Rafael, CA: Origin Press.

Phan Thi, K. P. 2017. *Fire Road*. Carol Stream, IL: Tyndale House.

Popenoe, D. 1996. *Life Without Father: Compelling New Evidence That Fatherhood and Marriage Are Indispensable for the Good of Children and Society*. New York: Free Press.

Potter-Efron, R., and P. Potter-Efron. 1989. *Letting Go of Shame: Understanding How Shame Affects Your Life*. Center City, MN: Hazelden Foundation.

Price, M., J. P. Connor, and H. C. Allen. 2017. "The Moderating Effect of Childhood Maltreatment on the Relations Among PTSD Symptoms, Positive Urgency, and Negative Urgency." *Journal of Traumatic Stress* 30: 432–437.

Raeburn, P. 2014. *Do Fathers Matter? What Science Is Telling Us About the Parent We've Overlooked*. New York: Scientific American.

Ridout, K. K., M. Khan, and S. J. Ridout. 2018. "Adverse Childhood Experiences Run Deep: Toxic Early Life Stress, Telomeres and Mitochondrial DNA Copy Number, the Biological Makers of Cumulative Stress." *BioEssays* 40: e1800077.

Rothschild, B. 2000. *The Body Remembers: The Psychophysiology of Trauma and Trauma Treatment*. New York: W. W. Norton.

Salzberg, S. 1995. *Lovingkindness: The Revolutionary Art of Happiness*. Boston: Shambhala.

Satchidananda, S. S. 2008. *To Know Your Self: The Essential Teachings of Swami Satchidananda*, 2nd ed. Buckingham, VA: Integral Yoga Publications.

Schiraldi, G. R. 2016. *The Post-Traumatic Stress Disorder Sourcebook: A Guide to Healing, Recovery, and Growth*, 2nd ed. New York: McGraw-Hill.

Schiraldi, G. R. 2016. *The Self-Esteem Workbook*, 2nd ed. Oakland, CA: New Harbinger Publications.

Schiraldi, G. R. 2017. *The Resilience Workbook: Essential Skills to Recover from Stress, Trauma, and Adversity*. Oakland, CA: New Harbinger Publications.

Schore, A. N. 1994. *Affect Regulation and the Origin of the Self: The Neurobiology of Emotional Development*. Hillsdale, NJ: Lawrence Erlbaum Associates, Inc.

Schore, A. N. 1997. "Early Development of the Nonlinear Right Brain and Development of a Predisposition to Psychiatric Disorders." *Development and Psychopathology* 9: 595–631.

Schore, A. N. 2003. *Affect Regulation and the Repair of the Self*. New York: W. W. Norton

Schore, A. N. 2009. "Relational Trauma and the Developing Right Brain: An Interface of Psychoanalytic Self Psychology and Neuroscience." *Annals of the New York Academy of Sciences* 1159: 189–203.

Schore, A. N. 2012. *The Science of the Art of Psychotherapy*. New York: W. W. Norton.

Shapiro, F. 2012. *Getting Past Your Past: Take Control of Your Life with Self-Help Techniques from EMDR Therapy*. New York: Rodale.

Shariful, A. S., and C. B. Nemeroff. 2017. "Early Life Stress, Mood, and Anxiety Disorders." *Chronic Stress* 1: 1-16.

Siegel, D. J. 1999. *The Developing Mind: How Relationships and the Brain Interact to Shape Who We Are*. New York: Guilford.

Singer, M. A. 2007. *The Untethered Soul: The Journey Beyond Yourself*. Oakland, CA: New Harbinger.

Sloan, D. M., B. P. Marx, D. J. Lee, and P. A. Resick. 2018. "A Brief Exposure-Based Treatment vs. Cognitive Processing Therapy for Posttraumatic Stress Disorder: A Randomized Noninferiority Clinical Trial." *JAMA Psychiatry* 75: 233–239.

Slobodin, O., Y. Caspi, E. Klein, B. D. Berger, and S. E. Hobfall. 2011. "Resource Loss and Posttraumatic Response in Bedouin Members of the Israeli Defense Forces." *Journal of Traumatic Stress* 24: 54–60.

Snyder, C. R., and S. J. Lopez. 2007. *Positive Psychology: The Scientific and Practical Explorations of Human Strengths*. Thousand Oaks, CA: Sage.

Speer, M. E., and M. R. Delgado. 2017. "Reminiscing About Positive Memories Buffers Acute Stress Responses." *Nature Human Behaviour* 1: 0093.

Steele, A. 2007. *Developing a Secure Self: An Attachment-Based Approach to Adult Psychotherapy*. CD and printed guide. Gabriola, BC, Canada: April Steele. https://www.april-steele.ca.

Syed, S. A., and C. B. Nemeroff. 2017. "Early Life Stress, Mood, and Anxiety Disorders." *Chronic Stress* (*Thousand Oaks*) 1. doi: 10.1177/2470547017694461.

Takikawa, D. 2004. *What Babies Want: An Exploration of the Consciousness of Infants*. DVD. Los Olivos, CA: Hana Peace Works.

Thompson, R. A. 2018. "Social-Emotional Development in the First Three Years." Edna Bennett Pierce Prevention Research Center, Penn State University. http://www.prevention.psu.edu/news/social-emotional-development-in-the-first-three-years.

Tinnin, L., and L. Gantt. 2013. *The Instinctual Trauma Response and Dual-Brain Dynamics: A Guide for Trauma Therapy*. Morgantown, WV: Gargoyle.

Tobin, R. L., A. L. Adrian, C. W. Hoge, and A. B. Adler. 2018. "Energy Drink Use in U.S. Service Members After Deployment: Associations with Mental Health Problems, Aggression, and Fatigue." *Military Medicine* 183: e364–e370.

Ulrich, W. L. 1992. "The Temple, Psychotherapy, and the Traditions of the Fathers." *Issues in Religion and Psychotherapy* 18: article 5.

Vaillant, G. E. 2008. *Spiritual Evolution: A Scientific Defense of Faith*. New York: Broadway.

van Bruggen, V., P. M. ten Klooster, N. van der Aa, A. J. M. Smith, G. J. Westerhof, and G. Glas. 2018. "Structural Validity of the World Assumption Scale." *Journal of Traumatic Stress* 31: 816–825.

Van der Kolk, B. A. 2014. *The Body Keeps the Score: Brain, Mind, and Body in the Healing of Trauma*. New York: Viking.

Van der Kolk, B. A. 2015a. "The Body Keeps the Score." Walden Behavioral Care Conference, October 29, Bentley University, Waltham, MA.

Van der Kolk, B. A. 2015b. "Developmental Trauma Panel." Changing the Paradigm 2015 Conference on Developmental Trauma: Where Trauma Meets Attachment, Echo Parenting and Education, March 5–6, Los Angeles, CA. https://www.echoparenting.org.

Van der Kolk, B. A. 2019. "Healing Trauma: How to Start Feeling Safe in Your Own Body." The *Science of Success* podcast with host Matt Bodnar, April 19. www.successpodcast.com.

Weinberg, M. 2013. "The Bidirectional Dyadic Association Between Tendency to Forgive, Self-Esteem, Social Support, and PTSD Symptoms Among Terror-Attack Survivors and Their Spouses." *Journal of Traumatic Stress* 26: 744–752.

Wilkinson, M. 2010. *Changing Minds in Therapy: Emotion, Attachment, Trauma, and Neurobiology*. New York: W. W. Norton.

Williams, M. B., and S. Poijula. 2013. *The PTSD Workbook*, 2nd ed. Oakland, CA: New Harbinger Publications.

Wolin, S. J., and S. Wolin. 1993. *The Resilient Self: How Survivors of Troubled Families Rise Above Adversity*. New York: Villard Books.

Worthington, E. L., C. V. O. Witvliet., P. Pietrini, and A. J. Miller. 2007. "Forgiveness, Health, and Well-being: A Review of Evidence for Emotional Versus Decisional Forgiveness, Dispositional Forgivingness, and Reduced Unforgiveness." *Journal of Behavioral Medicine* 30: 291–302.

Young-Wolff, K. C., A. Alabaster, B. McCaw, N. Stoller, C. Watson, S. Sterling, et al. 2019. "Adverse Childhood Experiences and Mental Health and Behavioral Health Conditions During Pregnancy: The Role of Resilience." *Journal of Women's Health* 4: 452–461.

Zeigler-Hill, V. 2011. "The Connections Between Self-Esteem and Psychopathology." *Journal of Contemporary Psychotherapy* 41: 157–164.

Zinsmeister, L. 1992. "The Murphy Brown Question: Do Children Need Fathers?" *Crisis*, October 1.

Glenn R. Schiraldi, PhD, has served on the stress management faculties at The Pentagon; the International Critical Incident Stress Foundation; and the University of Maryland, where he received the Outstanding Teaching Award in addition to other teaching and service awards. His books on stress-related topics have been translated into sixteen languages, and include: *The Resilience Workbook*; *The Self-Esteem Workbook*; *Ten Simple Solutions for Building Self-Esteem*; *The Post-Traumatic Stress Disorder Sourcebook*; and *The Anger Management Sourcebook*. Glenn's writing has been recognized by various scholarly and popular sources, including *The Washington Post, American Journal of Health Promotion, Mind/Body Health Review,* and the *International Stress and Tension Control Society Newsletter.*

He has trained laypersons and clinicians around the world on various aspects of stress, trauma, and resilience, with the goal of optimizing mental health and performance while preventing and promoting recovery from stress-related conditions. His skills-based mind-body courses at the University of Maryland have been found to improve self-esteem, resilience, happiness, optimism, and curiosity, while reducing symptoms of depression, anxiety, and anger. He has served on the editorial board of the *International Journal of Emergency Mental Health and Human Resilience,* the board of directors of the Depression and Related Affective Disorders Association, and the ABC News post-traumatic stress disorder (PTSD) working group. A graduate of the United States Military Academy, West Point; he holds a doctorate from the University of Maryland. He is founder of Resilience Training International, which serves people facing great stress, their families, and their helpers. Learn more at www.resiliencefirst.com.

Real change *is* possible

For more than forty-five years, New Harbinger has published proven-effective self-help books and pioneering workbooks to help readers of all ages and backgrounds improve mental health and well-being, and achieve lasting personal growth. In addition, our spirituality books offer profound guidance for deepening awareness and cultivating healing, self-discovery, and fulfillment.

Founded by psychologist Matthew McKay and Patrick Fanning, New Harbinger is proud to be an independent, employee-owned company. Our books reflect our core values of integrity, innovation, commitment, sustainability, compassion, and trust. Written by leaders in the field and recommended by therapists worldwide, New Harbinger books are practical, accessible, and provide real tools for real change.

 **newharbinger**publications